Dear Andy,

All the best success!.

Winning the Audit

12 Proven Steps to Achieve Successful Customer and Third-Party Quality Audits

Monika N. Ardianto

Winning The Audit
12 Proven Steps to Achieve Successful Customer & Third-Party
Quality Audits

Published by
10-10-10 Publishing
1-9225 Leslie St.
Richmond Hill
Ontario, Canada
L4B 3H6

For information about special discounts for bulk purchases,
please contact 10-10-10 Publishing at 1-888-504-6257.

Printed in the United States of America

ISBN: 978-1-927677-03-2 (Paperback)
ISBN: 978-1-927677-12-4 (Hardcover)
ISBN: 978-0-991760-11-4 (E-book)

To the most important people I have in this lifetime,

my son, Jordan,
my mom and dad, Nina and Soekamto,
and my husband, Andrew

They are my greatest inspiration and the reason
why I want to achieve
more and higher
in my life

Foreword

Go to any bookstore, and you will find there are many books written on the subject of auditing principles and techniques. However I would say there is rarely or perhaps none that is written to provide practical guidance for any company to be successful particularly at customer and third-party audit.

In today's business era, it is necessary to take all measures in order to stand out from other competitors. The obvious way to do that is by having a company management system that sticks out from the crowd. Many companies do not get into investing for quality – even though in my opinion it should be part of their budget to become a world class company. I do not blame them. Building an effective quality management system is a long term process and you need an expert to help you.

Monika Nonce Ardianto is a quality professional, certified quality auditor and certified quality manager by American Society of Quality, who knows what she is talking about. Quality management is one of the most important aspects in producing a consistent high quality product as well as in building a great company. If you ever have an opportunity to hear Monika speak or if you ever have the chance to be certified by her in ISO 9001 quality management system, grab it.

Monika is truly an expert in her profession. Her book *Winning the Audit* is a very important work in this field. It perfectly presents her skills, experiences, objectives and messages. *Winning the Audit* can help every company get qualified or certified by their customers or regulatory bodies. This tells me that if you want to get the job done, to ensure you have an effective quality management system, Monika is the best person to help you.

Monika's *Winning the Audit* helps quality professionals focus their accomplishments and provides clear direction on how to take the company to the next level. I am happy to say that I have no doubt that Monika's advice and career expertise are key components in allowing you and your company to make it to the top of the pile.

Raymond Aaron
New York Times Bestselling Author
www.UltimateAuthorBootcamp.com

Acknowledgments

Every worthwhile part of my life has been accomplished with the valuable help of many loving and incredible individuals – and the writing of this book is no exception.

I perhaps most grateful to my husband, Andrew, for encouraging me to attend an event that has led me to meet the New York Times Bestselling Author, Raymond Aaron, and learn about writing a book.

I am forever indebted to Raymond Aaron. He has shown me that writing a book is possible through his 10-10-10 Program. Without his guidance this book will never happen. And I thank him as well for his willingness to write the foreword for my book.

I am all for challenges, but a book seemed too big a project for me to push through. I realized this book would never have come together if I didn't have an amazing family to lean on. Andrew and my son, Jordan, who kept me rooted. Both of them gave the space and time to work, and were my inspiration throughout.

I owe a debt of gratitude to my parent, Nina and Soekamto, for their unconditional love. They give me a gift - a strong sense of responsibility to be successful and they believe in me intensely, holding the notion that I will become successful.

I am very fortunate to have Lori Murphy, the amazing personal book architect, who enthusiastically keeps me going on-track and encourages me to finish my book on-time. Her feedback always gives me high confident feelings that I will be able to finish it well.

I owe huge thanks to Wendy Almeida. Wendy is an editor extraordinaire who has powerfully helped me sort through, organized, and edited all of my ideas.

I am deeply privileged to have Dr. Mohamed Abousalem P.Eng., MBA, the CEO of TECTERRA Inc., Franklin Kurniawan Lim, the VP, Operations of Xenon Technologies Pte Ltd, and Brent Grazman, Ph.D., the VP of Quality of a leading multinational electronics manufacturer, for their willingness to write their comments on this *Winning the Audit* book. I thank them very much for taking their time, despite their busy schedules, to read and comment on my book.

I want to thank the staff at The Raymond Aaron Group, such as Ryan Malfara, Carol Lee, Joelle Mintzberg, Jennifer Le, and Lynn Moffatt who have helped me in their unique ways to make this book come to realization.

I am deeply honored to have around me friends, colleagues and fellow auditors who have made such valuable contributions to my life and to my work. This book to a large extent flowed out of their wisdom. Whatever I am able to learn from them, combined with my own wisdom in unique ways, is delivered through this book.

I have learned so much from the brilliant leaders and also owe a huge debt of gratitude to the companies that I have worked for, who have trusted me in helping them and their organizations grow, and for their unique contributions to the *Winning the Audit* model.

The spirit of the writing process has opened me up to so many new people and ideas, and I am extremely grateful to God for that.

Contents

Introduction:

In Praise of ISO 9001

> *The two words 'information' and 'communication' are often used interchangeably, but they signify quite different things. Information is giving out; communication is getting through. (Sydney J. Harris)*

Organizations face many challenges. Quality and environmental management, food safety, supply chain security, occupational health and safety, and information management are just some examples. More and more companies are turning to specific management system standards to help them meet such challenges efficiently and effectively. In today's business environment, customers demand assurance that their suppliers' activities are performed correctly and consistently and comply with numerous quality, safety, and regulatory requirements.

Many companies have sought and achieved certification or registration of one of the ISO 9000 standards. Other companies have wanted to become ISO 9001 certified but have been unable to afford the long-term costs associated with maintaining compliance or have been un-willing to go through all the necessary steps required by the ISO 9001 registrars or auditors.

So, what is so great about ISO 9001? Why would a company want to become certified in the first place? Is certification the only way to go?

Whatever your current thoughts may be, please allow me – as a professional experienced in quality management – to explain the fundamental benefits of ISO 9001 and demonstrate why ISO 9001 is the best management tool ever created.

When we look at how houses are built all over the world, there is one thing strong houses have in common: a good foundation. The better the foundation, the better the house will stand the test of time, regardless of how many families pass through its doors.

ISO 9001 has a robust set of guidelines, and if they are implemented correctly an organization can establish policies and procedures that allow business processes to continue for many years – a sound foundation for the company.

Businesses employ people who learn the company culture and idiosyncrasies and apply it to their own working habits. Employees who work in companies that do not follow or are not ISO 9001 registered typically use their prior experiences and try to apply them to their current jobs. Some will yield great results and some won't, but each experience will be different and there won't be common ground.

The ISO 9001 standard gives you the principles you need to have a solid foundation that can become part of your company culture.

ISO 9001 is a renowned international quality management standard. It is rapidly becoming the most popular quality standard in the world. According to surveys conducted by ISO:

- As of 2007, there were 951,486 certified companies globally; 25,000 of these companies are in the United States.
- As of 2009, China made a huge leap and became the country with the greatest number of ISO 9001 certifica-

tions issued. The country amassed 257,076 certificates (a quarter of all the ISO 9001 global certifications issued).
- As of 2010, the worldwide total of ISO 9001 certificates was 1,109,905; 36,632 of these certificates were issued to the companies in North America.

Many more businesses are in the process of becoming ISO 9001 certified. Why are they doing it? Because it controls quality. It saves and brings in money. Customers expect it and competitors use it.

ISO certification produces numerous benefits for a business, such as meeting customer requirements in a professional manner, attracting new customers, getting more revenue, promoting the company's brand, improving the company's procedures, and increasing customer satisfaction.

Nowadays, most companies prefer to do business only with those companies that are ISO certified. Therefore, ISO certification can help a company open up new markets it had no access to before certification.

When applied correctly, your employees will embrace the ISO 9001 approach and make it part of their business culture. If top management spreads and enforces this culture, it is very likely that every employee in the company will be directly or indirectly indoctrinated. This culture will then be transferred from employee to employee, senior employee to junior employee, senior staff to new hires. All employees will move in the same direction toward the same goals, becoming empowered and more secure in making the right decisions for the business.

When you become ISO 9001 registered, employees are proud of their quality management system. Sales and marketing people are excited and eager to place that "ISO 9001 Registered" logo on every piece of company literature. Although it may seem that sales and marketing are often the least interested group in getting the company ISO 9001 registered, their behavior changes when it's time to market their achievement.

The registration process, which seemed like a lot of work, is now a new tool to gain additional customers and a new reason for pride as existing customers are told, "We have a quality management system based on the ISO 9001 standard and we are proud of it."

The ISO 9000 family of standards is a blueprint outlining what organizations must do in order to implement and display good quality management practices. Taken into account are customers' quality requirements, applicable regulatory requirements, customer satisfaction, and continuous improvement in achieving these goals. The quality management system standard was created on the premise that satisfied customers are the lifeblood of an organization. If the organization wants to achieve high profits, it must keep customers satisfied. To keep customers satisfied, it must meet customers' requirements.

ISO 9001 applies to all types of organizations. It does not matter what size they are or what they do. It can help both product- and service-oriented organizations achieve standards of quality that are recognized and respected throughout the world.

If you already have a functioning quality management system but do not follow ISO 9001, I suggest that you carry out a gap analysis. A gap analysis will tell you exactly what you need to do to meet the ISO 9001 standard. It will help you identify the gaps between the ISO 9001 standard and your organization's processes.

If you don't have a quality management system or you are starting from scratch, I suggest that you use an ISO 9001 process-based quality management system development plan to develop your company's quality management system.

Once your quality management system has been fully developed and implemented, this book can help you to get ISO 9001 certified or qualified successfully. This book is designed to help a company that already has a quality management system to reach their benchmark faster.

Within this book, you have access to the unique sequence and method that has been honed, tested, and most important, proven to help many companies get qualified and certified by their customers and third-party auditors.

Here Is What You'll Learn

Step 1: Communicate and Create Powerful Message

This step presents communication strategies, techniques, and tips on getting top management and employee support. You will learn that your ability to provide your management and employees with the audit information they need, when they need it, in the format they need, is crucial to a successful audit.

Step 2: Prepare and Get Ready

In this step, you will learn unique processes to reveal what is important to you in order to effectively plan and conduct the internal audit and to get ready for customer and third-party audits. You will also learn how to focus your attention on moving toward what is truly important to a meaningful audit.

Step 3: Take Action Now!

This step teaches you the importance of taking necessary actions very soon after the audit and building a sense of urgency throughout the company.

Step 4: Build an "A Team"

This step demonstrates the magnitude of building a great team and becoming a great leader, which will enable you to achieve your goals successfully.

Step 5: Get Your Team Ready for the Audit

In this step, you are encouraged to ensure that your team is familiar with documents and procedures, be experts in their own areas, and understand the expected good behaviours during the audit.

Step 6: Create a Great First Impression

This chapter describes the significance of having a great first impression that immediately conveys to the auditors that you have your facility, quality management system, and manufacturing processes under control.

Step 7: Conduct an Outstanding Opening Meeting

In this step, you will learn how to plan and conduct an audit opening meeting that can serve as an opportunity to put both the auditors and auditees at ease, create a good impression of the company's systems and clean up any misconceptions right from the beginning.

Step 8: Remember: It's Showtime!

This step teaches you what you need to say and do during the audit in order to display to the auditors that you have your facility and processes under control and that you know what you are doing.

Step 9: Give Them Only What They Want

In this step, you will be given rules for preparing and gathering the information and documentation that will meaningfully support the achievement of the audit objectives.

Step 10: Be Cool

This step teaches you the value of building effective interpersonal skills and how to handle yourself during the interview that will contribute to the quality and success of the audit.

Step 11: Know Your Right to Fight

In this step you will learn that you don't have to accept all of the findings, and that you have appeal rights should you not agree with the audit findings and observations.

Step 12: Conduct a Memorable Exit Meeting and Audit Closing

This step presents unique and important techniques to plan and conduct a well-run closing meeting that will display professionalism and create an opportunity to maintain a positive relationship with the auditors. You will also learn to create recognition and compliment both auditors and auditees, which will make the next audit run smoother.

How This Book Can Help

> *Effective leadership is putting first thing first. Effective management is discipline, carrying it out. (Stephen Covey)*

The word "audit" is associated with formal or methodical examinations, reviews and investigations that are done by some professional groups. Third-party audits are totally independent of the customer-supplier relationship and may result in independent certification of a product, process, or system.

The responsibility for ensuring that any audit is successful in serving its intended purpose rests primarily with the audit program manager who plans and works on the audit requirements. *Winning the Audit* provides a step-by-step guide through the process needed to prepare for an audit, including establishing and maintaining a professional atmosphere, basic auditing techniques, auditors' etiquette, the most likely areas for discovering problems, common auditing pitfalls, communicating results, handling findings, and appropriate audit follow-up actions.

This book is also designed to provide practical guidance that will enable any company to achieve success on their regulatory or customer audit. It provides guidelines on powerful communication, getting top management and employees' support, conducting a powerful opening meeting, examples of audit situations, audit etiquette, and conducting a memorable exit meeting. Auditing is conducted by professionals; therefore, all individuals affected by an audit need to know how to conduct themselves in the professional manner demonstrated in this book.

Winning the Audit can be used by audit program managers, quality management representatives, quality managers, lead auditors, auditors, quality professionals, and management system consultants to gain an understanding of the practical steps toward achieving successful audits. Quality managers and company quality management representatives will find this book very useful as a guide for leading and managing their customer and regulatory audit program. This book can also be used by trainers and educators as source material for teaching best practices during auditing.

Winning the Audit is not designed as a standalone text to prepare for an audit. As with all audit activities, you are encouraged to work with the stakeholders or process owners in your company for successful preparation and execution. It is also important to use the *ASQ Auditing Handbook* in conjunction with this book.

Winning the Audit is organized to align with external audit sequences. There is a preferred sequence of activities that should be performed to conduct and achieve successful audits. It is common to refer to the steps of the sequence as communication phase, preparation phase, performance phase, report phase, closure and follow-up phase.

This book uses generic terms in order to support broad principles. Some situations provided as examples are based on experience and shared by the author as a means to add value to the text and provide clarity to the readers. Since many of the concepts and practices discussed are based on experience, the execution and implementation of each item is based on the situation at the time of the audit.

In a nutshell, all quality professionals will find *Winning the Audit* a very useful guide for leading and achieving successful customer and regulatory audits.

Step

1

Communicate and Create Powerful Messages

> *The art of communication is the language of leadership.*
> *(James Humes)*

Introduction: Communication Is Key

Communication is key to successful leadership. In fact, Lee Froschheiser, the president and CEO of MAP Consulting (MAP) and author of *Vital Factors: The Secret to Transforming Your Business - And Your Life*, states that having a clear communications strategy is the most important quality in great leadership.

Organizations use a wide variety of communications to relay information of all kinds to shareholders, employees, customers and the public. Communication plays such an integral role in business that some companies have internal personnel or departments to manage all internal and external communications.

Communicating Is Your Job

The quality of your success in audit depends directly on the quality of your communication with others. In that respect, communication is not *about* your work – it *is* your work. Your ability to provide your management and employees with the audit information they need, when they need it, in the format they need, is crucial to a successful audit.

While the messages themselves may be simple in nature, a great deal of planning and thought should go into how a message is constructed and delivered. You need to understand what makes a powerful message, how to develop a powerful message and, most importantly, how to deliver a powerful message. You need to engage all the senses – not just the mind – because powerful communication is not just *what* you say, but *how* you say it.

Create a Strong Communications Strategy

A strong communications strategy will ensure that your message is received and understood by your intended audience and it should include the followings important factors:

- **Your objectives and goals**
  Create a solid foundation for your message by writing down exactly what you want to achieve. Isolate the purpose and outline the key ideas you want to emphasize.

- **Your audience**
  Who are the recipients? Are they top management, employees, or the entire organization? Your audience will define your content and determine how your message is presented. For instance, a message you

send to all employees may include less technical information than a message you send to management.

- **A timetable**
  Establish a timeline for the event so that your audience is able to plan ahead to accommodate your resources requirement.

- **Evaluation and review**
  Determine that review and feedback will be provided once the event has been conducted.

A communications strategy encompasses all forms of communication. If you are in charge of your audit communication plan, choose from many types of media and methods to fit your message content and communication goals.

Clarify Your Audit Goals First

As Paul J. Meyer describes the characteristics of S.M.A.R.T. goals in *Attitude is Everything*, the first term ("Specific") stresses the need for a specific goal rather than a more general one. This means the goal is clear and unambiguous.

To make goals specific, they must tell a team exactly what is expected, why it is important, who is involved, where it is going to happen and which attributes are important.

When setting goals for an internal audit, ask the following questions:

- What do I want to accomplish?
- What are the specific reasons and purposes for accomplishing the goal?
- What benefits will the company enjoy by accomplishing the goal?

- What are the requirements and constraints?
- Who is involved?
- Who is the right person?
- Where is the location?
- When is it done?
- How many or how much?
- How will I know when the goal is accomplished?
- How can the goal be accomplished?
- What can I and others do today?

Customer or third-party audit objectives may be designed to:

- Maintain your customer's confidence in your company
- Verify your conformance to contractual agreements or requirements
- Certify the company quality program and/or management system
- Follow up on corrective actions

You can clarify the customer or third-party audit objectives by contacting and building good communication with your auditors or customer representative (usually someone from supply chain or quality management groups). Obtain the confirmed audit plan and schedule the audit so you have time to pre-screen and have adequate discussion with your upper management.

Of course, the ultimate goal of a quality audit from your company's perspective is to simply PASS the audit, become certified by the third party and/or qualified by the customer and improve your business results. Therefore, the message you want to convey to your customers or auditors is that your processes and systems are under control and you know what you are doing.

Make Your Content Specific

Information is the basis of all corporate communication and, in fact, the basis of all communication in general. Accurate information will provide a powerful message that leads to immediate attention and action.

Communication about the coming audit should include the following:

- The type of audit. Quality audits are generally segregated into system, process, and product audits.
- The customer or audit organization, auditor's name(s) and their titles.
- Applicable regulation and standards, i.e. ISO 9001, TL9000, ISO 13485, etc.
- Audit scope and criteria. This must be established for each planned audit. Is it statutory, regulatory, or based on contractual requirements?
- Calendar activities, audit date and schedule.
- Affected location(s) if you have more than one facility.
- Protocol and rules. For example, you may need PPE (Personal Protective Equipment) or a specific production coat.
- Outstanding action(s), if any.
- Reference documents (procedures, instructions, specifications, etc.), and where to find them.
- Goals, milestones and the importance of achieving them.
- Individual and team accountabilities.
- Where to find support and help. Provide contacts' names, email addresses and the specific assistance they offer.
- Necessary follow-up actions.

TIP: Remember, the clearer and more concise your message, the more easily it will be understood by your audience. If the necessary information will make your message too long, provide a detailed calendar and schedule as an attachment.

Communicate with Top Management and Get Their Support

Gaining top management support is crucial to the success of every business project. Top management commitment is the factor that makes the difference between success and failure when developing and implementing an audit.

True support involves more than getting a signature on the cheque. Top management need to rally the troops, get the word out that the audit is important to the company, and protect and support people when difficulties arise.

In order to get top management support and commitment, a separate pre-meeting with them is highly recommended. Use this time to go through the audit plan, objectives, goals, and resources needed. Let top management know what will ensure successful execution of the audit.

Be sure to argue the case for a "top-down force" rather than a "bottom-up pull". Explain why it is important for top management to attend the opening and closing meeting, to give an elevator speech on business management, or to conduct a company-wide meeting to explain the importance of the audit and the need to achieve the audit objectives.

Once you get the go-ahead signal, be sure to keep top management support and commitment by showing their names in the carbon copies (cc) list when you send communications about the audit plan, or state their names and any directions they have given in the body of the message.

Tips for Getting Top Management Support

While it may sound simple, getting and keeping top management support is not always straightforward. The fact is, audit is generally not the first thought in an executive's mind.

If you find it difficult to get management support for the audit, here are four techniques to try:

1. Show them the money. Talk to them in their language – dollars. Speak in terms of time wasted, material wasted, etc. Remind them that these all have a cost.
2. Show them how a successful audit will please a customer, which will lead to more dollars.
3. Show them that the audit is required by regulations.
4. Find someone in top management who actually gets the big picture and wants to do the right thing because it's the right thing.

Communicate Throughout the Organization and Get Their Support

People are key to the success of any organization. Therefore, working together as a team is essential to audit success.

As an audit team leader, you need to communicate that teamwork is the key to your business and that the business cannot accomplish its goals unless everyone in the company contributes to and has ownership of the audit.

Audit is a cross-functional project and the issue of gaining support from people outside your direct control is a common one. Most projects are staffed by people from several areas of the organization who rarely report to the project manager. They are, in effect, "borrowed" resources and they're usually "borrowed" from someone who already had plans for them.

One way to build support is to carefully connect the goal of your audit program to larger goals in the organization. You should be able to show how achieving your audit goal will help them achieve the goals of their own area. Using this method, try to develop a good connection with the people whose support you need. The closer the connection, the stronger your case when asking for support.

Try scheduling separate meetings with each key group to help them get started in terms of gathering necessary documentation. Make sure they clearly understand what's at stake if the audit is unsuccessful.

Foster a sense of togetherness and strong teamwork in any messages you send by specifying the people or teams who are accountable for achieving the audit goals.

Create Powerful Email Messages

The old school taught that good writing was wordy, heavy, complex, and academic prose. This style is no longer valid in the fast-paced world of the twenty-first century workplace, where virtually all professionals have too much to read and no time to waste.

Today's business writers should make their prose lean, crisp, dynamic, cogent and easy for busy audiences to grasp immediately.

Strategic message writing – writing that gets results – can be extremely powerful. Be clear about what you want your message to accomplish and stay focused on that purpose. Keep in mind your audience's needs, wants, and desires. Select your content based on why they need your information and how they will use it.

While email has revolutionized written communication in the workplace, too often corporate emails are a mess of jumbled ideas. They are either too long and packed with unnecessary information or too brief for clarity.

Email writing has its own art form. If it is done well, your audience gets your point quickly, knows what action you expect them to take, and is encouraged to respond with more information or better ideas. In other words, it doesn't waste their time and it moves the conversation along.

> **TIP:** When it comes to emails, simplicity is power.

Follow Best Practices for Email

Here are some best practices for creating and delivering a powerful email message:

- **The subject is the headline**
  Remember that the email subject is the first thing your audience sees, so grab their attention. Create a punchy, action-oriented or time restricted email subject. Think of the subject line as a "headline" that summarizes the content in three to five words. The subject determines whether your email gets read or not, so it should focus on what is in it for the audience. Besides making the subject relevant to your

target audience, it is also important to instil a sense of urgency or importance.

- **Get to the point**
  Online writing has to be kept concise and clear, largely because the screen is a particularly unfriendly reading medium for most people's eyes. You need to get straight to the point and keep to it. Keep your sentences short, simple, and only include one main idea or thought per sentence. Paragraphs should be no more than four to six lines. And if you list more than a couple of items, use bullet points. Remember that your email broadcast is only a means to an end. People want information quickly and clearly.

- **Generate excitement**
  Try to incorporate your feeling of excitement in your email and get your audience to share that excitement. Select promotional and motivational words to promote action.

- **Don't over design**
  Ensure that your entire message can be viewed on a single screen. Avoid using different font sizes and typefaces that only confuse and distract audiences from the main message. Layout of emails is something few people need to pay attention to, especially if their system uses text only. However, you should avoid writing emails that sprawl all the way across the screen. This makes it very hard to read and to see everything properly as text, and your audience may have to fiddle about changing fonts.

- **Learn email etiquette**
  Make the effort to learn about the etiquette (these days known as "netiquette") involved in writing emails. There are many sites online that can give you advice.

- **DON'T USE CAPITALS**

  Occasional use of capital letters to emphasize a word is ok. However, USING ALL CAPITALS IS DIFFICULT TO READ AND LOOKS AS IF YOU ARE SHOUTING. DON'T DO IT!

- **Call people to action**

  Tell people what you want them to do. Don't leave them wondering what to do next. Point them to your "most desired action". Also provide a reason to act NOW. People are in a hurry and they tend to have short attention spans. Let them know that they need to get involved now or they may miss their opportunity. Give them a compelling reason to take action NOW (sense of urgency, mandatory, outstanding problems, etc.).

- **Make it easy**

  This is the most important email broadcast rule. Always include a clear and crisp call to action (like "See attached" or "Go to the link") that allows users to access detailed information easily. Provide clear instructions on the actions you want your audience to take. Whether it is to call you, answer a question or go to your website, make all action steps clear and concise by telling them exactly what to do.

- **Spell it right and proofread**

  Think about the last time you received a marketing email with poor spelling and grammar. Will you buy their product? Typos make you look sloppy and lazy. Use auto spell check. But read it once more before sending, because spell checkers and their users have a bad habit of inserting the wrong word into the document.

- **Get the name right**
  Make sure you write and spell the recipient's name correctly. If you are not sure of the spelling of the auditors' or auditees' names and how they prefer to be addressed, take the time to find out.

- **Conclude**
  If you have a fairly long email, don't forget to repeat the call to action at the end. Although the audience may already know where to call you, including your contact information in the communication will be seen as a helpful addition to your message.

- **Follow up**
  You should not think of an email broadcast as a one-time hit. Set up reminders regularly at proper intervals. Follow up after sending the message to ensure the recipients have indeed received the communication and understand its contents. This accomplishes two things. First, it ensures that the message was constructed properly. Second, it gives the recipients the opportunity to ask any questions they may have about the message's content.

See the sample of audit communication email at the Appendix and visit my website www.winningtheaudit.com to explore the type of communication that fits to your requirements.

When to Communicate

If your audit is a customer or third-party audit, once you have gained approval from top management communicate your acceptance of the audit schedule and plan back to your customer or auditors.

You are now able to broadcast the news officially to all employees. If at all possible, schedule your communications as follows:

Communication	What	When
Communication #1	Notification	Not less than 2 months prior to the audit
Communication #2	Follow up, progress or closure of outstanding items	4 weeks prior to the audit
Communication #3	Reminder	1 week before the audit

Some people prefer to send a broadcast email in the morning between 6 am and 10 am. However, if your company has facilities and employees in different time zones, don't worry about your send times.

Remember, it is not the specific time that makes the recipient open and read the email. A result-oriented subject line and appropriate "From" name are much stronger factors when it comes to determining an email's success. It is powerful content that leads to the immediate actions required for a successful audit.

> **TIP:** A quality audit does not normally use surprise tactics. Surprise tactics are acceptable under at least two conditions: to verify that safety requirements are being met or when a dishonest activity is suspected (i.e. for Environmental Protection Agency - EPA, Food and Drug Administration - FDA, or health inspections).

Step 1 Summary

Here are the basic things you have to know and do to communicate and create powerful messages about the coming audit;

- Communication Is Key
- Communicating Is Your Job
- Create a Strong Communications Strategy
- Clarify Your Audit Goals First
- Make Your Content Specific
- Communicate with Top Management and Get Their Support
- Tips for Getting Top Management Support
- Communicate Throughout the Organization and Get Their Support
- Create Powerful Email Messages
- Follow Best Practices for Email
- When to Communicate

Step

2

Prepare and Get Ready

> *Spectacular achievement is always preceded by spectacular preparation. (Robert H. Schuller)*

Introduction: Always Be Prepared

The key to success during any audit is strategic and effective preparation. Auditors love hard work and preparation. It's wired in their audit brains and they really appreciate solid preparation.

Ideally, a company should be ready for a customer or regulatory audit at any time. Systems, documents and records should always be maintained in a compliant and "audit ready" condition.

Unfortunately, many companies fail to prepare adequately for customer or regulatory audits. Since an audit announcement can appear a very short time before the audit, it is imperative to develop a compliance mindset so your company is always ready for an audit.

Everyone in the company should continually ask the following questions:

- Am I prepared for a short-notice audit?

- Do my employees know how to conduct themselves during an audit?
- Am I confident in our ability to respond to difficult questions related to our processes?

Internal auditing is a tool that company can use to locate, eliminate, and prevent problems *before* the customer or the regulatory agency does. Companies need to be agile and responsive to changing requirements from their customers or markets because once customers or certifications are lost, it is very difficult to recover. This is one reason why internal audits are recognized as an important asset to manufacturing or service industries.

A properly directed regular internal audit program can help your company achieve its objectives, stay focused, and uncover new improvement opportunities.

The Importance of Internal Quality Audits

Simply put, quality audits are performed to evaluate the quality of a system. It is important to conduct self-inspections, or internal audits, to ensure compliance with the requirements or standards. If non-conformances are noted by an external auditor that were not identified during internal audits, the external auditor may conclude that both your quality system and measures taken to monitor the performance of the system are weak and ineffective. This would be a very undesirable audit outcome.

An effective internal audit program is one that achieves its objectives via processes that are capable and efficient.

Unfortunately, many managers and executives have low expectations of audit programs. They view an audit program as nothing more than the cost of ensuring compliance to regulations. Once you as the audit program manager demonstrate how effectively the audit program supports the organization's objectives, your upper management will start to see that an audit program can add value beyond compliance for the company.

It is the job of the internal quality auditor to carry out the tasks of the audit, comply with requirements, respect confidentiality and perform due diligence by collecting evidence about system quality. These observations should then be documented and acted upon in order to maintain the integrity both of the process and the audit. Should the process need to be refined, auditors must record this as one of the follow-up actions.

An internal audit should be done right and it should be done professionally.

> **TIP**: When conducting an internal audit, do it as if you were competing with your competitors and could lose the business if you don't do it well.

Develop an Internal Audit Plan

During an internal audit, your company uses its own auditors. No outside auditors are involved. The internal audit is mostly performed by in-house personnel who have been trained in auditing principles.

To effectively plan for and coordinate an efficient and timely internal audit, clear lines of communication need to be established early in the audit process.

When developing an internal audit plan, consider the following areas:

- Define the scope: understand the specific areas to focus on

- Plan the audit: good planning will lead to a successful audit
- Define an appropriate schedule: the right timing can make all the difference
- Organize the team: coordinating your team's efforts will ensure a more efficient process
- Communicate with auditees: an informed auditee will lead to better results
- Execute: conduct the internal audit according to the plan

Establish Standards, Focus and Scope

When planning the internal audit, determine what standard is to be used as a basis for comparison in your examination. If you will be using official standards and requirements, published criteria or industry practices, be sure that you are thoroughly familiar with the criteria and any and all policies regarding their interpretation and application.

Be sure of your footing. You don't want to tell the auditee one thing and then have the customers or regulatory auditors cause you to change your interpretation. Likewise, you don't want the auditee to find you lacking in knowledge of the criteria.

Be realistic about what you can accomplish in the time allowed. Restrict the scope to those areas that appear to offer the best prospects for accomplishing the purposes of the audit. If there are too many of these, give consideration to performing more than one audit.

Once you are at the auditee's site and have started your examination, you can expect to be able to further narrow and refine the scope as you eliminate those areas unworthy of in-depth review and discover new areas worth pursuing.

Create a Strategic Plan

An important part of the process for managing an internal audit function involves strategic planning. For successful audits, again you first need to know what you want to achieve (audit objectives), then determine what procedures you should follow (audit methodology), and assign qualified staff to the audit (resource allocation).

Once you know the focus and scope, you can start developing strategies to achieve the internal audit program objectives. The strategies will be based on your organization, your culture and its resources.

Some of the strategies and tactics you use may include:

- Developing an enhanced customer-focused process, such as a call centre, that collects feedback from customers. Such a process is vital to learning what works and what doesn't work, as well as identifying customer needs.
- Identifying any corrective actions that are already closed or still outstanding.
- Developing quick guidelines or technical support manuals.
- Verifying the company KPIs to ensure you stay on track. KPIs should be quantifiable measurements that are agreed to beforehand.
- Adding value by reviewing department or area objectives and performance.
- Verifying claimed improvements by the functional departments and reporting your findings to top management.
- Reducing audit areas by demonstrating continuous compliance or decreasing audit frequency as supported by compliance reports and real-time data (compliance indicators based on performance).

- Establishing a network of audit advisors for areas that need assistance to comply (based on past results).
- Considering the possibility of outsourcing for more cost-effective oversight.
- Implementing a program to schedule audits based on changes in processes or key personnel. This will help you to identify and prevent non-compliance issues before an external audit.

One goal of your initial planning should be to establish a starting date for the audit. You may propose and discuss the date with management or specific department heads. However, although you may have established your organization's timing needs and deadlines, you will need to coordinate those schedules with your internal auditors to ensure that there are no conflicts.

Establish an Audit Schedule

The best practice to establish an audit schedule is to contact the auditees and their management and determine the best time to conduct the on-site portion of the audit. Be sure to take into consideration both what you need to see and the auditee's operational restraints. If possible, let the auditee select the time(s) for the audit – that way his organization will be more committed to giving you the cooperation you need.

The audit plan and schedule should be presented to and reviewed by your management for their approval. Internal communication about the audit schedule needs to be sent out to all employees once approval is obtained. Any auditee's objections should be resolved between the audit team leader and the auditee and his/her management (if necessary) prior to the audit.

See the sample of quality audit plan at the Appendix and visit my website www.winningtheaudit.com to explore the type of plan format that fits to your requirements.

Involve Your Team

The planning stage of an audit may entail some team meetings to gather and exchange information. The objective of this stage is to divulge all information necessary for the auditors to coordinate a successful audit. A thorough knowledge exchange is key to avoiding the problems that arise when an auditor discovers something that was not known at the planning stage of an engagement.

It is always a good idea to develop the plan with your audit team. The plan should focus on detailed milestones and deadlines for each team member to meet. The milestones will provide a blueprint for the preparation of the reports that support your achievements in the audit.

Before the audit, the team should gain an understanding of the auditable business units and their operations, as well as any unique characteristics or business practices. To begin, the audit team should review any relevant work documents or records from the prior year, as well as any applicable standards.

The initial planning meeting will also be an opportunity for the auditee to meet the audit team.

Work with Auditees for an Effective Internal Audit

For an effective internal audit, the auditor and auditee should take the following steps in preparation for the audit.

- **Perform a pre-audit review**

  With a little effort on your part and early cooperation from the auditee, you can learn a tremendous amount about the auditee's facility and program long before you set foot on site.

- **Review procedures**

  Get copies of the auditee's procedures that cover the planned scope of your audit. Obtain up-to-date copies of these procedures and review them carefully to get the flavor of the auditee's program. When you visit the auditee's site, you may find some differences between how things are done and how the procedures say they are done. This is not necessarily bad – it is simply a fact of life. This is where you can provide value-added advice to the auditee and management.

- **Review performance data**

  Depending upon the scope of your audit, the auditee may be tracking and analyzing performance data that you can review to determine trends and to identify areas for further examination.

- **Review previous audits**

  Look at any available reports from previous audits of the specific auditee. You will be most interested in those audits performed recently. Keep in mind that the older the information, the less likely that it is still valid. You should strive to be informed about these previous audits, but you should not let them influence your decisions when you conduct your own audit.

Develop Internal Audit Checklists

Almost all organizations today need a high-quality ISO management or environmental management system audit. You need to establish an audit program that results in thorough, effective, and uniform audits.

Audit checklists, based on lists used by internal and external auditors, is an important tool to help build an effective audit. The use of checklist questions is instrumental in guiding the audit team. It will help to keep you and the audit team focused on the audit's purpose, scope, and objectives.

Many times employees at all levels in the company become "uptight" or experience some kind of "audit anxiety" regarding ISO registration or long-lasting proficiency audit by their registrar. Fact gathering and the use of ISO audit checklists can help avoid this anxiety.

A well-organized audit checklist will provide an excellent starting point for your audit. Your goal here is to guide your internal auditors as they perform their work. Additionally, an associated document folder may be dedicated for the audit team to file their work so that every team member is able to view the audit progress. Following your direction, they can also refer to reports from last year's audit file to gain preliminary knowledge.

To assure that the appropriate and necessary questions are asked and that evidence is examined where needed, you should send the checklist questions to the auditee at the same time you send the formal individual audit invitation.

See the sample of internal quality audit checklist at the Appendix and visit www.winningtheaudit.com to explore other checklist that fits to your needs.

TIP: It is worthwhile to put in a little bit of extra effort to ensure that all items have been assembled, and assembled properly. This stage is an important one. A number of issues can be avoided by simply performing a quality review of the audit checklist and other audit documents during the last few days leading up to your audit.

Create a Quality Audit Invitation

If possible, build your email Outlook invitation so it can display on a mobile phone.

Here are some tips for creating an audit invitation that will engage participants and boost their enthusiasm for the audit:

- Write a subject line with a call-to-action or a sense of urgency.
- Provide all event details in the email. If you are using an email invitation template, this will be included automatically.
- Pitch your participants. Give a reason they won't want to miss this opportunity.
- Customize your invitation by including the audit checklists and references or supporting documents or files.
- If sending a link, make sure it is clickable and accessible.
- Keep it short.
- Re-send to non-responders.
- Include an agenda so people have an idea of the topics that will be covered.
- Include the name of the room or area for the audit.

- Provide the date and day of the event. Double check! (How often do you see Wed. 4th Feb. only to find that Wed. is actually the 5th. Which one is correct?)
- You may want to add your signature to your email invitation.
- Monitor for email bounces or fails and decide what to do about them.

Once the critical information is dispensed with (and this should all be on the first screen), don't forget to attach or provide a link to more detail for those who want to keep reading. Provide them with the procedures, checklists, presentation, or other related documents.

> **TIP**: The next time you get a great email invitation, stop and think about why it has appealed to you and see if there are some lessons you can learn. This is one of the best exercises of all.

Select Internal Auditors

The success of the audit depends heavily on the lead auditor (team leader). As the audit team leader, you must have extensive training covering the principles, applications, and conduct of auditing practices. You also must have good oral and communication skills, interpersonal skills, be honest, and have good organization and management skills.

Employees chosen as your permanent audit team members should possess the same characteristics.

Based on the *ASQ Auditing Handbook*, make sure you ask your audit team to apply and uphold the following principles:

- **Integrity**
  Establish trust and provide a basis for relying on your own judgement.

- **Objectivity**
  Exhibit the highest level professional objectivity. Make a balanced assessment of all the relevant circumstances and don't be influenced by your interest or by others in forming your judgement.

- **Confidentiality**
  Respect the value and ownership of information received and do not disclose information without appropriate authority, unless there is a legal or professional obligation to do so.

- **Competency**
  Apply the knowledge, skills, and experience needed in the performance of the internal audit.

All of the internal auditors must, at the very least, be aware of the ISO 9001 standard and its requirements. In total, the ISO 9001 standard contains 52 different compliance requirements, which in turn include about 135 ``shall statements", with an expectation that you must comply with all of them.

You need to ensure that employees are actually complying with the standard's requirements and create an infrastructure that allows them to do what they need to do.

Dos and Don'ts for Internal Auditors

Internal auditors represent an independent set of eyes supporting the insight that is needed in our fast-paced world economy. When you arrive at the auditee's site, you must know exactly what you are going to do and how you are going to do it. Your time in the field is too valuable to be wasted on unproductive preliminaries.

Regardless of how well you may know the auditee and his facility, always begin the on-site portion of your audit with an entrance meeting. Let the auditee determine who should attend the meeting, but be sure to include your main point of contact for the audit.

If the auditee has made any concessions or special arrangements for your visit, be sure to thank him for his cooperation. If the auditee wants to give you a guided introductory tour of his or her facility, don't turn him down (especially if upper management will be conducting the tour).

Don't be in too much of a hurry to start what you consider to be "productive" work – give the auditee time to adjust to your presence, and give the auditee's upper management a chance to demonstrate their support for the audit.

Internal audit team members should always conduct themselves in a business-like manner and maintain as low a profile as possible.

The following table will show what are the Dos and Don'ts for the internal auditors;

DO	DON'T
• Listen actively and avoid lecturing or speaking in a manner that might be construed as condescending. • Keep your conversations to the point and avoid being excessively friendly or chummy. • Conduct your examinations discreetly, and be polite and courteous to all of the auditee's employees. • Follow and adhere to all rules and procedures established by the auditee. • Leave the area or the facility when requested to do so by the auditee.	• Joke about the audit or the auditee. • Manipulate controls or operate equipment. • Offer suggestions for action on a problem unless specifically requested to do so by the auditee. • Ask the auditee to deviate from or otherwise violate any procedure, rule, or regulation. • Discuss the audit with personnel who are not involved in the audit.

Six Methods of Gathering Information

The secret to conducting an effective audit is to know how to look, where to look, and what to look out for. There are six basic methods of gathering information in an audit. You should use each as it best suits the type of information that you want to obtain, but you should never rely on just a single method.

- **Interview**

  Always be certain you are talking with the right person to provide the desired information. A one-on-one discussion is easier to focus and control. Keep your questions open-ended and do not dominate the discussion. Interview whenever and wherever you get the chance – as you inspect and observe, as you review records, as you conduct exercises, and even as you debrief the auditee.

- **Inspection**

  When conducting an inspection, proceed from the general to the specific. First, get a good overall view of the facility, room, piece of equipment, etc. Next, examine prominent features and, finally, specific items. Ask questions as you inspect, starting with general inquiries on purpose and function and then more specific ones on how the item is produced or used. Keep your eyes and ears open, and avoid focusing too tightly on any single attribute.

- **Observation**

  Often the easiest way to learn how a process or system actually works is simply to watch it work. Many routine activities and special operations will provide opportunities for you to see personnel working together in as close to normal circumstances as you are likely to find. For example, if you want to examine ESD (Electrostatic Discharge) control practices, you could stand at the ESD wrist trap tester point at a specific time when you might be able to see how the staff follows the ESD rule requirement.

- **Records review**

  Make a random sampling of the records for a given area.

- **Tracing**
  This consists of following a specific evolution from beginning to end (trace forward) or end to beginning (trace backward). Normally this is done by tracking the records that are created in the process.

- **Exercise**
  Auditors can also run exercises on a much smaller scale to test an auditee's programs, personnel, and equipment. Such exercises are tests that the auditee normally performs on a routine basis. However, as the auditor you need to pick the times and circumstances for the tests with the knowledge and cooperation of the auditee.

Identify Potential Problem Areas

There are certain aspects of any program or facility that are more likely to develop problems than others. When your audit's purpose is to identify problem areas, you can aim at the following targets and be fairly certain of finding something worth pursuing;

- **Old procedures**
  Check the approval and revision dates on important written procedures. If a procedure has not been revised within the last two years, or if it was written and approved by individuals who are no longer on the auditee's staff, the chances are good that the procedure is out of sync with the process or system. The significance of this problem will depend on how much reliance is placed upon written procedures in the auditee's process.

- **Old facilities and equipment**

  Any facility, instrument or equipment that appears old in relation to current technology may indicate a problem area. Your audit might show that the system is not capable of performing the required process or that it is a bottleneck in the internal production.

- **Temporary fixes**

  When you come across a situation that the auditee claims is temporary, find out just how temporary it really is and whether or not the original problem has been solved or merely hidden.

- **Complex programs**

  Any process, procedure, or system of getting things accomplished that appears to be quite complex normally has some "unofficial" shortcuts associated with it (counter to what management may believe). In the worst cases, these shortcuts will involve serious departures from approved procedures and possible unsafe practices. In the best cases, the shortcuts may be beneficial improvements that should be implemented officially.

- **Department interfaces**

  There are always rivalries and communications problems between departments on the same site and between corporate and plant groups. These often lead to inefficiencies in any work that requires the cooperation of the different groups.

- **Unrealistic requirements**

  A policy, procedure or method that appears to be too strict or lax in relation to its objectives usually warrants further review to establish its merits. Your audit might reveal that the requirement was valid at one time, but that it has not been changed to reflect current conditions, or that the requirement was an overzealous response to a previous incident.

Focus the Internal Audit

To give you an easy audit trail, you want to focus the internal audit on the following:

Top Management
- Identify the processes needed to achieve the organizational goals and determine how these processes interact.
- Develop an organizational policy and objectives.
- Establish the Key Performance Indicators (KPIs) needed to measure performance against the objectives.
- Ensure that the resources needed to manage the system are available.
- Conduct a management review meeting per conditions outlined in the ISO 9001 at least once a year.
- Communicate company developments to all employees.
- Demonstrate that the Key Performance Indicators (KPIs) are measured, evaluated and communicated.

Quality Management Representative
- Ensure that the quality management system documentation is sound and current, and that changes to the system are approved before they are implemented.
- Ensure that relevant versions of applicable documents are available at points of use.
- Ensure that the company auditors are adequately trained.
- Develop an audit schedule and conduct audits of all system procedures.

- Demonstrate that the corrective and preventive action processes are working.

Human Resources
- Verify that all employees have a basic understanding of the ISO 9001 quality management system.
- Establish qualification criteria for all of the administrative and operational job functions.
- Prove that all employees, including top management or executives, meet their job function qualifications.
- Establish a training program for developing employee skills.

Sales and Customer Service
- Demonstrate that customer feedback, including complaints, is gathered and analyzed.
- Prove that processing capabilities are reviewed before orders for new products are confirmed.

Purchasing
- Demonstrate that all primary vendors are qualified and that their performance is routinely evaluated.
- Prove that material specifications are verified before they are released to vendors.

Engineering and R&D
- Demonstrate that the information released to production is current, accurate, and complies with customer and applicable statutory and regulatory requirements.
- Show that product changes affecting form, fit or function are implemented with approval either from customer or authorized parties.
- Demonstrate that the critical performance characteristics are verified and validated before product changes or new products are released to the market.

Planning

- Demonstrate that the capacity to make the product or provide the service in accordance with the order's terms is available.
- Prove that you provide the personnel responsible for making the products or providing the services with the information needed to fulfill the order's terms.

Production

- Establish a calibration program that complies with the standard's requirements.
- Demonstrate that the equipment and machinery capabilities have been verified and validated.
- Prove that nonconforming materials are not mixed with conforming materials.
- Confirm that shipments comply with customer requirements.
- Prove that incoming materials comply with purchase specifications.
- Demonstrate how materials with a limited shelf life are managed.

Don't Go Alone

It is recommended that you have other auditors go with you as a team during your visit to the auditee's site. Discuss your progress with them and get their ideas on the significance of what you find and the approaches that you can take to further evaluate areas and reach conclusions. Be sure to take advantage of their experience and their different viewpoints.

Alert your team to information you need that they may come across in their own investigations. If you report back to a main office during a break in the audit, you can run your preliminary conclusions by other members of the team and get additional input. But remember, while other auditors' opinions are useful, you are still the one who has to do the work, and are the only one who is responsible for your conclusions.

Ask Thought-Provoking Questions

Too often we don't challenge ourselves by asking the hard questions of our management or peers because we want to avoid rocking the boat or don't want to look like we're checking up on how somebody does his or her job.

Try a different tactic. Ask thought-provoking questions – not to intimidate the auditees, but to help them set new benchmarks.

During the internal audit, auditors generally ask the following universal questions:

- How do you know what to do?
- Can you show or tell me how you do it?
- How do you know when it is done right?
- What do you do when it is not done right?

Here are some thought-provoking questions that may be asked of auditees:

- How do you satisfy your customers?
- Does the technology help you measure customer satisfaction? Can you please describe it?
- How do you select and recruit your customer service personnel?
- How do you select potential locations or markets to expand your business?
- How do you evaluate a trainee's performance?
- How do you stand out from your competitors?
- How do you keep your edge?

- What government regulations affect the industry and company?
- Why does this particular process exist?
- How does this process offer value to the customer?
- Why are there so many steps in the process?
- Why do we need to have multiple decision loops?
- Why are there so many headcounts required for this process?
- Is this process created for legacy systems to work around limitations of those systems or justify past headcounts?
- How do you determine whether controls are adequate?
- What drives change in the company?
- Which of the company's greatest challenges or problems have not been fixed yet? What is the strategic plan to fix them?

Dealing with Difficult Auditees

Occasionally you will come across an auditee who is extremely defensive and uncooperative. There are three possible approaches to dealing with such an auditee:

- Empathize with him and attempt to gain his trust
- Go around him by dealing with his coworkers or subordinates
- Pull rank on him by pointing out his uncooperative attitude to his superiors

As long as such auditees represent isolated cases, they should not have any appreciable effect on your ability to conduct an audit. If, however, an uncooperative attitude is being fostered by top management, you may find it necessary to obtain assistance from the authority for the audit.

Don't attempt to conduct an audit in an overly hostile environment. Instead, let the authority negotiate for a more reasonable approach with the auditee or his/her management.

Tips to Avoid Common Auditing Pitfalls

There are many traps that await the unwary auditor in the rush to complete the full scope of an audit. Here are some tips for avoiding common auditing pitfalls:

- Don't pass judgment until you are reasonably sure of your facts. When you do reach a conclusion, fly it by the auditee in a debriefing session to get his reaction. You may be surprised to find that you have misinterpreted what you saw or that you have forgotten to examine a crucial piece of evidence.
- Not every individual on the auditee's staff is or should be knowledgeable of all aspects of a program. Do not expect complete knowledge from any particular auditee. If you expect to obtain a complete understanding of any program, you will have to talk to more than one person and collect information by more than one method.
- Don't restrict yourself to examining only one side of the story. Check with internal suppliers and customers also.
- Don't waste your time examining areas that are clearly outside the scope of your audit or your authority. Likewise, don't bother with those areas that are obviously not going to yield any significant results. Once you feel that you have collected sufficient evidence on a subject to support your conclusions, stop and move on to the next item. Don't let the auditee lead you into an unproductive quest for data that you don't need and won't use.
- Eventually you will come across an individual who has been eagerly awaiting a chance to complain about

the ills of the company or management. You should search for the grain of truth in what he has to say by asking for specific examples and by verifying these with information that you obtain from other sources.

- It is all too easy to examine only those areas that you particularly like to review or for which you are uniquely qualified, or repeat the same routine from audit to audit. Don't let your predisposition or past auditing experience dictate your approach – treat each audit as a separate and unique case.

- Keep the auditee informed of your basic impressions. Tell him what you think is good, what you think is bad, and why.

- Don't allow yourself to become a part of either the problem or the solution. The auditee is responsible for the solution, not you.

- No matter how stupid the error, keep emotion out of your criticism – make it constructive, not destructive.

- Some auditees will try to influence your conclusions to support points that they may be trying to win with management or with another auditor. Don't accept the auditee's interpretation of the facts – draw your own conclusions. It is all right if you agree with the auditee, but don't go out of your way to represent the auditee.

- Never accept any type of verbal assurance or "gentlemen's agreement" from an auditee over a problem area. The auditee may have good intentions at the time, but he also may not be able to obtain the management support necessary to fix the problem if you omit it from your audit report.

- Be very cautious if the auditee does not raise any serious objections to your conclusions during the audit. He may be waiting until the final exit or report presentation to discredit you. Don't fail to get his honest reactions to your conclusions before you finish the audit.

Aim for No Surprises

It's quite simple. If there is bad news, the potential for bad news, an unhappy customer or auditor, an accounting error, a software bug or the like, we want to hear about it first from the people closest to us. How embarrassing is it to get information from the auditor on a critical issue that you knew nothing about but should have?

The "No Surprise Rule" should encourage your team to effectively communicate to you without the fear of becoming the messenger who gets shot, or getting unduly chastised for making a mistake.

Employees or managers who don't make mistakes are not learning very much and probably only doing low value tasks. As Oscar Wilde once said, "Experience is simply the name we give our mistakes."

Here is what you can do to implement the No Surprise Rule:

- Encourage your team to tackle initiatives on their own. Let them know that you are supportive and available at any time to provide advice.
- When your people come to you with bad news, indicate to them that you appreciate hearing about it sooner rather than later and that they have done the right thing.
- Practice this same rule yourself. Never surprise your team or management with your findings, especially if they are related to critical areas. This is particularly true for employee evaluations.
- Provide continual feedback and follow-up.

Implementing the No Surprise Rule will improve effectiveness and trust among team members.

Keep Good Records

A good auditor must have a well-organized approach to taking, reviewing, and refining his notes. During interviews you should take written notes as unobtrusively as possible. Record key points, but don't be elaborate.

Your audit checklist can be very useful for note taking, especially if you have taken the time to jot down some of the questions that you plan to ask. At the earliest opportunity after an interview, you should go over your notes and fill in any details that you did not have time to record. Don't tape record interviews – you'll find that you won't do as good a job at interviewing when you aren't forced to take notes.

During observations and exercises, try to avoid the appearance of being overly concerned with your note taking. Each time that you write something down the auditee will think he has done something wrong. If you are writing continuously, the auditee will become nervous and frustrated by your silent judgment of his actions. Limit your note taking to key items only, and then fill in the details from memory at a convenient time afterwards.

Another occasion for a good memory arises whenever you tour or inspect contaminated areas. You can't take notes while you are dressed in protective clothing, so you'll simply have to develop a mental note-taking technique.

The notes that you do take are worthless unless you use them to organize your thoughts and to help you reach conclusions about the system, process or product you are auditing. You should review your notes at the end of each day, compare them to your audit outline, and rewrite or expand upon the notes as necessary to get the facts to fall into a logical pattern.

Each time that you do this you are, in effect, replaying the audit in your mind – you will discover new relationships between the facts and you will find out where you need to obtain more information to complete your analysis of the facts.

Preparing for Independent Third-Party Audits

Independent third-party auditors from regulatory agencies or registrar bodies have objectives to ensure an organization complies with statutory and regulatory requirements. Some third-party auditors believe that the audit will also improve ongoing compliance, as well as effectiveness.

To ensure effective audit preparation, you may want to contact the auditors to verify and reconfirm which areas, locations, processes or products are within the audit scope.

For third-party audits, you should verify that the following items are included:

- last company audit report
- corrective action request
- claimed improvement
- changes in the company objectives
- changes in the process
- changes in the system
- changes in the organization chart
- changes of major supplier or contract manufacturing
- changes in the database system

Preparing for Customer or Certification Audits

For customer qualification or certification audits, you may need to verify with the management and business development group which specific process or product the customer would like to verify. It may be for a new product agreement, an original equipment manufacturing contract, a significant increase in the business agreement, entering a partnership, or a pre-award survey.

When planning the internal audit for the purpose of preparing for a customer audit, you should also consider obtaining background information on:

- customer's contract or agreement
- supplied products
- any non-conformance or returned/repaired products
- any customer complaints and corrective action requests
- customer appraisals
- customer properties
- forecasts
- sales
- Return of Investment (ROI), etc.

Step 2 Summary

The key to success during any audit is strategic and effective preparation. Here are the principal steps you have to execute and familiar with to get you and your team ready for the audit;

- Always Be Prepared
- The Importance of Internal Quality Audits
- Develop an Internal Audit Plan
- Establish Standards, Focus and Scope
- Create a Strategic Plan
- Establish an Audit Schedule
- Involve Your Team
- Work with Auditees for an Effective Internal Audit
- Develop Internal Audit Checklists
- Create a Quality Audit Invitation
- Select Internal Auditors

- Dos and Don'ts for Internal Auditors
- Six Methods of Gathering Information
- Identify Potential Problem Areas
- Focus the Internal Audit
- Don't Go Alone
- Ask Thought-Provoking Questions
- Dealing with Difficult Auditees
- Tips to Avoid Common Auditing Pitfalls
- Aim for No Surprises
- Keep Good Records
- Preparing for Independent Third-Party Audits
- Preparing for Customer or Certification Audits

Step

3

Take Action Now!

> *Procrastination is the grave in which opportunity is buried.*
> *(Unknown)*

Introduction: Don't Procrastinate!

Highly productive people and companies seem to share a common trait that makes the difference between average and superior performers. This common trait is a sense of urgency.

It is important to take necessary actions very soon after the audit. Most people would rather decide what they think is best than be told what to do. As an audit program manager as well as team leader, you know that using your authority is not always the best way to generate actions, and often it does not work.

Building a sense of urgency does work. It drives people and companies to work much harder than normal. It makes people work as if their lives depend on it (which, in many cases, is true).

Communicate Findings – Now!

Communicating the results of the audit to management and employees is one of an auditor's principal responsibilities. We are measured on how effectively we report to all levels of management on problems needing management's attention. Each of your reports must therefore be well planned and carefully prepared to ensure that all important items noted in your examination are promptly and properly brought to their attention.

Officially tell the auditee, the auditee's management, your organization, the authority for the audit, and any other interested parties what you found as soon as possible. You must inform the auditee right away and should inform management no later than 48 hours after the audit.

If your findings require immediate top management attention, make an official report within the same day.
You must be able to clearly communicate your conclusions to sometimes diverse groups, both orally and in writing. You must also be able to "sell" your conclusions to the auditee and your own organization. Your goal should be to provide sufficient information and to interpret the information as necessary so that every party in the audit will be able to take proper actions, whatever they might be (e.g. measures, corrective actions, criteria changes, etc.).

Whether or not you are a professional writer, it benefits you to write in a professional manner. Conveying a clear message is vital, especially if you want to obtain resources or persuade others. If you don't write clearly, you will confuse the audiences and waste their time.

Begin the Formal Audit Report – Now!

The formal audit report is the product of the audit. As the team leader, you are responsible for its content and accuracy, and for submitting the formal report in a timely fashion. After arriving back from the audit, the work of the formal audit report should begin immediately while audit details are still fresh.

Written audit reports are our usual means of communicating because:

- They represent our formal, official position on the results of our audit work and our suggestions for action.
- They provide us with a basis for setting our own report standards (in quantity and quality) against which we can measure our audit effectiveness.
- They receive wider circulation at higher levels of management and, therefore, greater and more serious attention than oral reports.
- Effective follow-up on corrective actions is, for all practical purposes, impossible unless what we have to say is included in an audit report.

The problem with formal report procrastination is that the longer it is put off, the less interested the auditee and management will be in pursuing corrective actions.

A late-arriving formal written audit report sends a signal to the auditee and upper management that this is apparently not as important as it was initially believed.

To avoid any such situations, you should complete and submit the formal internal audit report as soon as possible within a week. With current technology, it is very possible to produce and distribute an audit report within 24 hours of the completion of the exit meeting.

There are many variations of the formal internal audit report. When writing the report, you should include at least the following:

- Cover sheet. Title of the report, date of issue, distribution list, standard, affected location(s), and executive summary.
- Main body of report. The main body contains the audit purpose, scope, auditees' names, audited locations, dates of the audit performed, audit team members and leader, and any functional information as necessary.
- Findings and observations.
- Request for corrective actions.
- Signature of the team leader is a must. (Signature of the audit team is optional.)
- Signature of audit authority serves as the report approval.

Report Audit Findings

Audit findings are a written explanation of errors, weaknesses, deficiencies, adverse conditions, or the need for improvements or changes that are disclosed in an audit. It is a constructively critical commentary on actions or inactions which, in the auditor's judgment, hinder the accomplishment of desired objectives in an effective and efficient manner. An audit finding usually is accompanied by a recommendation for specific action to correct the cited deficiency.

During each phase of the audit (i.e. preliminary survey, systems understanding, and fieldwork), potential findings should be documented on finding sheets or audit checklists, whichever you use for your record. The auditor-in-charge should discuss the findings with the department head (via meeting, phone call, e-mail, etc.), and document discussions on the finding sheets or on the audit checklist. At the conclusion of each phase, findings will be reviewed by the team leader.

Although each finding is different, the basic characteristics of an audit finding are as follows:

- It must be significant.
- It must be based on accurate information.
- It must be adequately developed in an objective manner and fully supported in the working papers.
- It must be based on sufficient evidence that supports the conclusions reached.
- The conclusions reached must be logical and reasonable and convincing.

You need to list each finding, in order of importance, with the supporting observations shown beneath it. Any requests for corrective actions may appear in the closing remarks, along with the date of expected response.

Report Noteworthy Accomplishments

Normally, audit reports concentrate on informing management about things that call for corrective action (findings). But you should keep in mind that particularly good operations may, under certain circumstances, be commented on in audit reports. Such comments must be adequately supported just as in the case of adverse findings.

It is suggested that noteworthy accomplishment should be reported in the final audit report. Auditees are expected to perform well, and you should acknowledge those who are doing an exceptional job and commend them in writing. This includes a description of the situation and how it affects the company quality program.

You should also mention if the auditee was cooperative, antagonistic or unsupportive. This information is important because it may be useful to the company, management and future auditors.

Contain and Correct It – Now!

Request for corrective actions is often presented in a separate standardized form. Whatever form is used, be sure it has a tracking number, which serves as cross reference.

The common format is:
- The findings or discrepant condition
- Affected standard or procedure
- Affected area(s)
- Process owner
- Response due date

Some of the corrective actions plan may require a considerable amount of time for the auditee and management to implement. It is best to give two to four weeks for an auditee to respond to a corrective action request. But remember that this does not mean that the auditee will necessarily have the plan fully implemented at that time.

Provide Recommendations

Generally, audit findings will result in one or more recommendations. Here are some good suggestions on providing recommendations:

- A recommendation should be specific, realistic and constructive. In addition, the recommendation should relate to the cause of the weakness or deficiency.

- Direct the recommendation to the specific auditee who has responsibility and authority to take corrective action.
- Avoid general recommendations (e.g. that controls be strengthened, that detailed plans be devised, that steps be taken to comply, etc.) unless you can combine such language with specific suggestions.
- Do not recommend action that has already been taken. Instead, report that corrective action has been taken.
- Avoid use of extreme language such as "immediately" or "expedite" unless the nature of the problem is so serious that such language is appropriate.
- Do not introduce new information (i.e. material not included in the "Audit Finding" section) into the recommendation. The recommendation should follow logically from what you present in the finding.

Get Commitment from Top Management

Audit findings should be discussed (via meeting, phone call, e-mail, etc.) with the department head, and results of the discussion should be documented. During the discussion, the auditor-in-charge should determine whether the department head concurs with the findings and recommendations. In addition, you or the audit team should consider revising the finding sheet based on the results of the discussion.

The auditor-in-charge should submit the filled-in and updated finding sheet or audit checklist to the team leader.

If a finding suggests the possibility of fraud or irregularity, the auditor-in-charge should obtain the team leader's approval or escalate it to the audit authority before discussing the finding with the department head.

Follow Up and Closure

The auditee and his or her management are responsible for developing and implementing the corrective action plans. Based on the established documented procedure for corrective and preventive action, the plan is developed by the auditee. This plan should clearly identify the necessary improvement activities and the target dates for full implementation.

Before closing the audit, the auditor-in-charge should verify that the permanent corrective actions address the root cause and strive to eliminate it, and have been effectively implemented.

See the template and sample of the internal quality audit report and result communication at the Appendix and visit my website www.winningtheaudit.com.

Step 3 Summary

In order to build up the sense of urgency of the coming audit, here are the vital steps you need to act;

- Don't Procrastinate
- Communicate Findings – Now!
- Begin the Formal Audit Report – Now!
- Report Audit Findings
- Report Noteworthy Accomplishments
- Contain and Correct It – Now!
- Provide Recommendations
- Get Commitment from Top Management
- Follow Up and Closure

Step

4

Build an "A Team"

> *Players win games, teams win championships. (Bill Taylor)*

Introduction: The Importance of Building an "A Team"

In every workplace, people talk about building a team and working as a team. However, few understand how to develop a successful and effective team, and some do not even have the experience of team work. True teamwork gives team members a feeling of being part of something larger than themselves.

A good team needs a good leader – and a great team needs a great leader. In a work situation, the leader is usually chosen by people outside the team. Presumably, you are already in this position or aspire to reach the position of team leader.

Becoming a great leader and building an A team has a lot to do with your understanding of the mission or objectives of your organization. It also has to do with creating a very good relationship between you as the team leader and your team. You and each member must recognize that every team member has his or her unique capability and that by working together and using the right approach, you will be able to achieve your audit goals.

Tips for Building a Great Team

Your ultimate goal in building a great team is not to ensure that every team member is great, but to ensure that collectively they will be great.

As the team leader, you have to harmonize, consolidate and synchronize each team member's efforts and blend them so the team's synergy will directly translate into superior team performance. This takes time and is sometimes difficult, but the achievement is well worth the work.

And don't forget – your most important mission is to improve results for your customers.

Here are some powerful actions you can take to build a great team:

- **Have a clear goal to achieve**
  Show your team a clear mountain top. Team members will come together when they feel they have some bold mission to achieve. A clear goal will not only evoke the best from the team, but it will inspire them to roll up their sleeves and work together to reach that goal.

- **Give 80% of your attention to your team**
  The growth and empowerment of the team is very important for a successful audit. Communicate and discuss every item that relates to the audit and value their input. Give the team 80% of your attention and reserve the remaining 20% for yourself and management.

- **Praise publicly but coach privately**
  This is one of the most important interpersonal skills required from great leaders. Great leaders understand the power of publicly praising excellence in ac-

tion. So do it often. On the other hand, coach your team members in private on the areas where they need improvement.

- **Do fun things together**
  Teams come together through shared experiences. It's important to do activities with your team members that allow them to show more of their true selves and connect with each other. Try to set up fun, creative and effective team meetings.

Develop a Talent Pool

Having the right people on the audit team is a key to success. So where do you find these people? By developing a talent pool.

The talent pool in any company is a group of high-performing and high-potential employees who are being developed to assume greater responsibility in particular areas. These employees form the basis of best-practice, talent pool-based succession planning.
To create a talent pool, you need to identify the knowledge, skills and experience that are critical to success in each area and critical to the organization's success.

The internal audit process provides an excellent way to identify talent. Interview current high performers in each area, as well as their managers. You might want to use a list of critical tasks or job responsibilities to begin your interviewing, and then move on to identify the key competencies required. Make sure you create detailed behavioral descriptions of those competencies and provide examples of what exemplar performance looks like.

To select the right people for the audit, you will need to work closely with HR, as well as prospective team members' managers and colleagues.

Who should be assigned to a talent pool?

- High performers: employees who are high performers in their current roles.
- High potential employees: people who have been identified as having the potential, capacity and interest to advance in the organization and broaden or deepen their knowledge, skills and expertise.
- People who embody the organization's culture and values. Many say this is most important, because you can teach technical skills, but not culture and values.

The next step is to choose employees in the talent pool to become your auditee team, the team that interacts with the auditors.

Integrate Your Team

After you have established your team, you will need to conduct a meeting to integrate them.

Interpersonal understanding and trust is critical in the process of building a great team. The group must be aware of each member's skills and personality. When a group is first formed, it's smart to hold a launch meeting that has 1-2 minutes at the beginning of the meeting for introductions, socializing, and to share ideas and information.

Members can get acquainted with one another as you start hammering out the team goals and creating a shared vision of success. Take time to share work progress and personal reflections. This will help fortify the group's understanding of each individual and how together they all contribute to a common goal.

To showcase their skills and experiences, members may take turns in the meeting sharing a past success or crucial lesson.

Achieving compliance means a lot of additional work for the team, so building effective and regular communications as well as good interrelationships among the team is important. Don't assume others know or think what you think. Work hard at communicating clearly and concisely. Work harder than you really believe is necessary. Keep everyone in the loop and give promised feedback. Last but not least, remember the power of simple courtesies like saying "please" and "thank you".

Select Presenters and Meeting Participants

After selecting your auditee team members, it is time to select and define who is going to present and participate in the entrance and exit meetings. Before selecting participants, ask yourself the following:

- Who is involved with this subject?
- Whose authority do we need?
- Who will be interested?

Work closely with your upper management and functional managers in the selection process. Not all team members need to be at entrance and exit meetings. The most important participants are the decision makers, such as top management or management representatives, the authority of the audit, the functional managers of the areas that are going to be examined, and some key staff appointed from the auditee team.

Make sure your team members are aware if they need to participate in both entrance and exit meetings. If some of them need to provide a presentation during the entrance meeting, let them know ahead so that they have adequate time to prepare their presentations.

Designate a Host Team

For an external audit, it is useful for you to define routes through the facility during the "audit tour". Work with functional management to designate the 'hosts' for each area. The hosts should be the selected auditee team plus co-workers who can help them during the audit.

When determining size and composition of the host team, consider:

- Objectives, scope, criteria, and audit duration
- Overall team competence
- Applicable statutory, regulatory, contractual, and accreditation/certification requirements
- Audit team independence and avoidance of conflict of interest
- Ability to interact and work effectively with auditees
- Language, social, and culture issues, experts, etc.

To prepare your hosts to answer auditors' questions, you may want to prepare some mock questions that the auditors are likely to ask.

Communicate Your Goal

Great leaders almost always strive for a singular objective. A winning organization might set a goal to win their top or major customers.

Your goal here is simply to PASS the audit with zero to minimum non-conformances and/or be awarded a contractual agreement with the customer. Make this goal known and understood clearly by the team and the whole company.

Inform your upper management and the auditee team that the message you want to display during the audit is that you have your facility and process under control and that you know what you are doing.

Foster Accountability

Accountability is a term often used in the workplace. The word accountable means responsible and answerable.

Audit team leaders are expected not only be accountable for results, but also for building a high-performing team and for the functioning of that team. In the process of holding the leader accountable, the team will be held accountable too.

A key component to accountability is expectations. We want people to fulfill our expectations and believe they should be held accountable for meeting or not meeting these expectations. It is very difficult for an organization to perform up to its potential without having a system of accountability as one of its basic practices. Even though most organizations and individuals hold the belief that we all need to be accountable, much of the time organizations do not know how to make this belief a reality.

Again, you need to be sure your upper management, functional managers and the team are clear about your objective, your goal, and your expectation of them for the audit. Make it clear what you need from them in order to successfully achieve your goal.

Another key component to creating an accountability culture is making sure you spend as much energy on rewarding those who are achieving their goals as you do correcting those who are not. This is something that is very often overlooked. People tend to notice when others are falling short, but take it for granted when they are accomplishing their goals.

If the accountability message comes from those in leadership positions in an organization, it will run throughout the organization and create an accountability mindset in each individual.

However, if one supervisor holds his or her staff accountable and another chooses not to, the organization will spend much of its energy dealing with this inequity. Time spent in this manner is time lost in moving the organization ahead towards achieving its goals.

Team accountability needs to be clear. Accountability must begin at the top and run through the entire organization and its culture.

Communicate with Participants

You may use an Outlook invitation or alike to provide some written invitation notification that will serve as a reminder to all meeting participants. The meeting invitation needs to include a statement of the purpose of the meeting, agenda, date, schedule and location.

Giving additional details may encourage participants to contribute much more productively. For example, if they have reports or data available that might be useful, participants should be requested to bring them. If they are expected to do a presentation they should be given time to prepare.

Participants also need to know of any special arrangements such as "Lunch will be served at ...." It is also useful to send participants any reference material that will help them prepare, such as report of the previous audit, corrective actions taken and recommendations or company overview.

As the meetings will cover several issues within a fairly limited time, agendas are essential. Use your agenda to keep your meeting moving forward. If non-agenda issues are introduced, insist the discussion will be placed at the end of the agenda. Use your agenda as a guideline and schedule to keep your meeting moving forward.

Step 4 Summary

To build an "A Team" here are the fundamental steps you have to comprehend and perform;

- The Importance of Building an "A Team"
- Tips for Building a Great Team
- Develop a Talent Pool
- Integrate Your Team
- Select Presenters and Meeting Participants
- Designate a Host Team
- Communicate Your Goal
- Foster Accountability
- Communicate with Participants

Step

5

Get Your Team Ready for the Audit

Coming together is a beginning; keeping together is progress; working together is success. (Henry Ford)

Introduction: The Importance of Training Your Team

Once you've selected and integrated your team, you need to prepare them for the audit. They will need to be familiar with relevant documents and procedures and understand how to conduct themselves in front of an auditor.

Understand Audit Techniques

It is a good idea to train your auditee team on the different audit techniques that an auditor may use. This will help them be more proactive and allow them to anticipate the next step in the audit process. Introduce to them the techniques likely to be used for the coming audit, such as:

- Trace forward: start with the raw material and follow the production flow
- Trace backward: start at the final product of a specific batch and go backwards
- Random: start at any point

Regardless of their level, respect your team members and value their input. Explain why they are participating on the team and how important their contributions are to the achievement of corporate goals.

> **TIP**: Time spent helping your team figure out how the company's internal processes and structures work will significantly contribute to the achievement of the audit objectives.

Review Relevant Documents

Prior to an audit, ensure that your team has reviewed any documentation that an auditor is likely to request. Make sure the documents are accessible and that all circulated documents are 'controlled copies' and up to date.

According to ISO 9001:2008 quality management system standard, there are six procedures required to be documented and maintained. They are:

- Control of documents
- Control of records
- Internal audit
- Control of non-conforming products
- Corrective action
- Preventive action

Typically, the auditor will review the following documents before arriving on your site:

- Quality management system manual
- Organization structure (if the auditor is new to your site or there were significant changes)
- Previous audit findings and your responses
- Recalls, complaints and adverse events

Know Your Key Procedures

The following procedures are regarded by auditors as key quality management system procedures to examine. Make sure that these procedures are current, that they adequately detail your processes, and that they are maintained and controlled. Be mindful that the deviation and change control registers (logs) may be used by the auditors to focus their audit activities.

- Design and development
- Calibration
- Handling temporary deviation
- Out of specification (OOS)
- Corrective action and preventive action (CAPA)
- Change control
- Release of product
- Competence, training, and awareness
- Preservation
- Supplier and contract manufacturing management and control

Know What You Need to Know

Below are some of the things every auditee should know prior to any type of audit.

Understand your processes
- Know who gives info/material/WIP/ finished product to you
- Know to whom you give your info/material/ WIP/ finished product

Understand your controlled QMS documentations
- Know your quality manual
- Know the procedure(s) pertinent to your job
- Know your work instruction(s)
- Know your form(s)
- Know who keeps your records (filled out forms) and where
- Know your quality policy
- Know your quality objectives

Understand who your management and support personnel are
- Know your company quality management representative (commonly shown in the organization chart)
- Know the main person in charge of any critical or major processes

Know the answers to common audit questions
- Can you describe your job responsibility?
- Who is your internal supplier?
- Who is your internal customer?
- Can you walk me through your process?
- How do you know if your work is good?
- What do you do if you find a non-conformance?
- Can you show me evidence?

Establish Dos and Don'ts

There is some basic behaviour expected of you and your team. Be sure you communicate these expectations to the entire team.

Good behaviour during the audit (Dos)
- Be courteous, cooperative, and professional
- Assist the auditors with their specific requests
- Answer only the questions asked by the auditors
- Be concise and brief
- Be polite and positive

Bad behaviour during the audit (Don'ts)
- Don't be rude
- Don't spring any surprises on the auditor
- Don't volunteer unrequested information
- Don't take too long to answer the question
- Don't say "I don't care", "I'm too sick and tired", etc.
- Don't be obstructive or argumentative
- Don't say something when being given the "silent treatment" from the auditor
- Don't provide answers to a question not related to the area of your responsibility or expertise, especially when your knowledge may be limited

Avoid Common Mistakes

There are some common mistakes made by auditees that are not recognized as mistakes at all until it is far too late to take corrective action, and may not be seen until the auditors present their findings. Here are the ones you and your team need to guard against:

- **Granting unescorted access**
  An unescorted auditor is an uncontrolled auditor. Auditors are strangers to the company. They don't know your facility, and they will not understand half of what they see if there is no one accompanying them to explain things.

- **Allowing the auditor to violate etiquette**
  Do not tolerate an auditor who fails to abide by the normal operations and safety rules. If the auditor interferes with your personnel, remove him from the facility.

- **Failure to keep management informed**
  If you don't report problems to your upper management as they occur, you will likely lose what management support you have.

- **Arguing in the presence of your management**
  Never have a confrontation with an auditor when your superior is present. You will embarrass your superior and you may lose his support.

- **Failure to show concern**
  When an auditor points out a minor problem that is easily corrected, you need to fix it immediately and report the resolution to him. Thank him for bringing it to your attention. Failure to take action on the easy problems may lead the auditor to believe that you may not be concerned enough about larger problems.

- **Failure to follow up**
  If you are unable to answer a question or if an auditor requests information that is not readily available, be sure to supply the answer or the information as soon as possible. Treat these "un-answers" as your own mini-findings that must be corrected before the audit is complete.

- **Questioning the standards**

  Arguing against the official standards will get you nowhere. The auditor is not in a position to change those
  standards, only to interpret them (on a very limited basis). Save these types of arguments for the formal responses to the findings.

- **Criticizing the auditor**

  No matter how dumb you may think he/she is, never directly criticize the auditor or his organization. When he is
  wrong, tell him that the situation might need further
  study, but don't tell him that you think he's unqualified to
  judge your quality program.

Step 5 Summary

Understand and train these critical aspects to your team in
order to get them ready for the audit;

- The Importance of Training Your Team
- Understand Audit Techniques
- Review Relevant Documents
- Know Your Key Procedures
- Know What You Need to Know
- Establish Dos and Don'ts
- Avoid Common Mistakes

Step

6

Create a Great First Impression

> *How you come across to others is too important to be left to chance.*
> *(Phil Geldart)*

Introduction: There Are No Second Chances

Whether in personal or professional life, people say that the first impression is everything. A great first impression can create a positive opinion in the minds of the people we meet, especially new people.

In business, from the minute someone walks through your doors, they begin to form their opinion of your company. If a good first impression is created, that impression will stick throughout the relationship. That's why it is important to immediately convey to the auditors that you have your facility, quality management system (QMS) and manufacturing processes under control.

There are no second chances for first impressions and it is crucial that the first impression the auditors get when they arrive on-site is a good – or, even better, great – one!

Cleanliness Counts

First impressions are made in seven to ten seconds, and can be exclusively visual until the auditors get to know you and your company.

Perhaps the first thing that gives people the right impression is cleanliness. A clean office is a happy office.

The front door is your guests' first impression of your business, so a clean front door leading to a clean and orderly waiting room or lobby will contribute to making the all-important first impression a positive one.

Businesses must also have a clean workplace, as well as clean washrooms. Visitors are easily discouraged when they come across a business that operates from an unsanitary, untidy location. Customers, in particular, are less likely to want to do business with a company that does not have clean facilities.

The importance of making that great first impression applies to every part of your business. So take the correct steps to represent your business in the best light.

Welcome Your Guests

Welcoming guests is an ancient virtue. The art of hospitality, or welcoming guests, is a revered practice in many cultures. It is important to put guests at ease as they enter your facility. Something like a friendly welcome sign can make a great impression at the curb or outside the lobby door and let guests feel welcome even before they enter the building.

Remember, the first thing your guests see upon entering the facility will set the tone for the day. Make a fabulous first impression with a welcome sign or other strategic message that suits your audit.

Remember the Receptionist is a Big Contributor

The receptionist is usually the first representative of a company that auditors or clients interact with. Having a smiling, polite and knowledgeable person at the front door is a great way to demonstrate to guests just how dedicated your staff is.

Receptionists are renowned for being on time and prepared for everything, even the smallest thing. A good receptionist is always ready to put stuff away or dust off a few things to make everything look in tip-top shape for whoever decides to drop into the office and say "hi."
One of the first things that a good receptionist will ask a visitor is, "Would you like coffee or water to drink? Or do you need anything else?" Having someone in the office who insures that clients are well taken care of is vital. Receptionists are truly at your service.

When planning the strategy for a customer or third-party audit, be sure to brief the receptionist on what needs to be done during the audit. This includes ensuring that he or she understands the company's vision, mission, quality policy and quality objectives. This may seem like overkill, but some auditors do ask questions about these subjects the first time they speak to a receptionist.

Arrange a Friendly Meet and Greet

But wait! Is there spinach in my teeth? This question is probably one you should always ask before meeting someone, especially important people. While you are at it, check your clothing and shoes for neatness, appropriateness and cleanliness.

When the auditors enter your facility, greet them with a smile, a friendly handshake and a brief introduction. The simple gesture of smiling at the auditors will make them feel at ease and create a comfortable ambiance between the two of you.

If you are wearing a clipped ID badge, it might be good to wear it on your right so that when you shake hands the guests' eyes will follow your arm up to the name tag and then your face. This helps them associate your face with your name. The badge should have both your first and last name, if possible, and the first name should be in large letters.

At this time, you should be able to verify the auditor's credentials. Exchanging business cards may be done at this time as well. Proceed to introduce any of your accompanying associates. For example, you might say, "Mr. Important Guest, I'd like to introduce you to our Engineering Director, Mr. Mike Callahan."

Show eagerness when you welcome the auditors. Step out of the door to welcome them upon their arrival, and offer to help them with any luggage they are carrying. Offer them a glass of water or coffee.

Focus on your guests and their needs. If you talk about yourself, do it sparingly. Train yourself to be a good listener. This makes a huge difference in building a relationship with a customer or regulatory auditor.

Taking genuine interest in them and their lives also goes a long way in demonstrating a genuine welcome. But be sure to take the cue from your guests in terms of how much they want to talk about themselves, or how much they are inclined to share.

Make sure you keep smiling. Smiling shows confidence, sincerity and approachability. And it does not cost a thing.

> **TIP**: Security personnel will most likely check the identification of the auditors, ensure that they register in the visitor's book and provide them with appropriate ID badges. However, it is up to you to make sure the auditors' names and company are spelled correctly.

Don't Forget IT Support

In many organizations, Help Desks are becoming the central area for end user support. When our computers function correctly, easily and properly, everything seems OK. But when things go wrong, it can drive us crazy. In this case, technical support from the IT department is very important. Typically, this encompasses computer hardware and software support. Certainly we can fix minute errors, but with major failures technical expertise is needed urgently.

Prior to the audit, engaging a dedicated Help Desk might be a good idea. Highly qualified and knowledgeable staff and experts working on the Help Desk should stand by to ensure the needs and wants of customers or auditors are met as they arise.

Step 6 Summary

To create a great first impression and positive mind set of the people you meet, you must be aware with these important factors;

- There Are No Second Chances

- Cleanliness Counts
- Welcome Your Guests
- Remember the Receptionist is a Big Contributor
- Arrange a Friendly Meet and Greet
- Don't Forget IT Support

Step

7

Conduct an Outstanding Opening Meeting

> *Organizing is what you do before you do something so that when you do it, it is not all mixed up. (A.A. Milne)*

Introduction: The Importance of Starting and Finishing Well

No matter what type of audit you are involved in, it is essential that it starts and finishes well. Opening and closing meetings offer the forum to do this. You need to think carefully about your agenda and approach to these two meetings, as they will constitute the auditors' first and last impression of the audit.

For auditors, the initial meeting at the start of an audit (the entrance or opening meeting) and the final meeting to wrap up the audit (the exit or closing meeting) represent two of the most important formal interactions with the auditees. Each of these meetings provides an opportunity to demonstrate and communicate key achievements. Therefore, they must be well planned.

Regardless of how well you may know your customer or auditor, always begin the on-site audit with an entrance or opening meeting. A well-run and professional opening meeting sets the scene for the audit and, if done well, creates a great first impression.

The opening or entrance meeting represents the first chance to meet the auditors in a formal setting. The opening meeting also gives the auditors the opportunity to establish a good audit environment, which will facilitate the smooth running of the audit. This meeting can serve as an opportunity to put both the auditors and auditees at ease, create a good impression of the company's systems, and clear up any misconceptions.

Tips for Conducting Opening Meetings

As the team leader, you will chair the opening meeting, so it is up to you to ensure the right topics are covered and that the auditors walk away with an adequate understanding of the company management and the auditees' work.

Here are some tips for conducting opening meetings:

- Prepare properly
- Ensure that the meeting is held in a suitable place
- Have a clear agenda
- Use time carefully
- Confirm that the program is still OK
- Clarify the role of any facilitator(s)
- Be professional

Prepare the Opening Meeting Carefully

Few would argue that conducting successful meetings is an essential skill in today's business environment. From introductory speeches to refreshments, a well-planned meeting will help your guests feel comfortable, respected and appreciated.

Prior to the auditors' arrival, you should have determined who will attend the meeting and discussed your agenda and who will participate in the meeting with your auditors.

The opening meeting should include senior management and any key staff that may be involved in the audit. During this meeting, the scope of the audit will be discussed. The time frame of the audit should be reconfirmed, and you should discuss any potential timing issues (e.g. working shift, lunch time, break time, end of shift time) that could impact the audit.

The content of the opening meeting is likely to include:

- Introduction of the lead auditor, their team and their company
- Introduction of you and your audit team
- Confirmation of the audit scope and objectives
- Presentation and brief discussion of the audit plan
- Discussion of the methods and procedures to be used during the audit
- Discussion of communication links for the audit
- Confirmation that resources and facilities are available
- Establishing a tentative time and date for the closing meeting

During the opening meeting, you should also advise the auditors about:

- Company policies on health, hygiene and safety
- Company policies on photographs, video and sound recording (auditors may be allowed to collect such evidence when deemed necessary)

- Normal operating hours (e.g. 8 am to 5 pm) and/or shift working hours
- Time for lunch and breaks, etc.

Because we are often pressed for time, you should set a firm exit meeting date or time for the conclusion of the audit. Providing this information will focus everyone on the importance of efficiency and effectiveness during the engagement.

During the opening meeting, you also need to establish the audit facilitator who will accompany the auditors throughout the whole audit. The facilitator might be you or your appointee. He or she will be the main contact should any information or escalation be needed during the audit.

Remember, relationships may be very formal at this point; therefore, you may want to hold the opening meeting in the board room.

Welcome and Introduce Your Guests

Whenever you are organizing a business meeting, showing proper respect and kindness to all of your guests ensures your event will be a success. Welcoming distinguished guests, however, requires more planning and attention.

During the opening meeting, you may want to do a round-table introduction of the individuals involved. This is an opportunity to make a good impression on both the auditors and senior management. Introduction points might include:

- Describing how and when you came to work at this company
- Sharing two things about yourself that you think no one at the table may know
- Sharing a great achievement and something you appreciate about your company

- Relating your plans for further development and improvement

Make Sure Your Agenda Is Clear

As the chair person, you must control each audit meeting if the audit is to go as planned and be effective. This is best achieved by issuing an agenda and explaining the audit plan to everyone involved.

Present the auditors with a clear agenda that outlines meeting times and locations, activities, participants and organized meals. A facility tour may be needed prior to conducting an individual audit. Familiarize the auditors with the facility and be sure to introduce the auditors to associates you bump into during the process.

Have a hard copy of the audit agenda handy for the auditors so they will always be prepared for the next activity.

No Tardiness

Be prompt, if not early – always. You can look sharp and professional, but if you can't make it on time, nothing else matters. This sounds easy, but too often the importance of punctuality is overlooked. Remember that being on time is crucial for audit success!

Here are some tips to ensure that you will arrive on time for the audit:

- Know exactly when you need to be at the office and subtract ten or fifteen minutes to establish your arrival time. This will give you time to go to the restroom or chat with colleagues. If the auditors are arriving at

7:45 am, you should arrive at the office by 7:30 am and be ready at the meeting area at 7:40 am.

- Listen to traffic news. If you depend on public transportation to get to work, always keep an eye on scheduled interruptions.
- Have a backup plan for your transportation. If you normally ride to the office with a friend, think ahead and plan what to do if your friend gets sick.
- Set up a reminder on your calendar. Outlook reminders are great and can be used to keep track of important events such as audits and meetings
- Set your clocks forward by ten minutes. This is a little psychological trick that many people play on themselves. The funny thing is, it really works!
- Remember: your reputation is on the line. The power of showing up on time is limitless. Don't fool yourself into thinking nobody notices the latecomer.

Lateness is corrosive to good relations with work colleagues. Even if you have a strong personality and can smooth over instances of lateness, tardiness still leaves a building resentment in others – particularly auditors who are prepared to work.

> **TIP:** Commit yourself to being 15 minutes early for *everything*. If you have to be to work at 8:00, don't even tell yourself this. Just tell yourself and everyone else who listens, "I have to be at work at 7:45." (But try not to annoy them or make them think that they are late or early!) If you do this, you will be on time even when there are unforeseen interruptions. You will be on time even with a traffic jam. And on those rare times that you actually show up 15 minutes early, you will get kudos for being an enthusiastic employee. You can also

chat with others who are early, and that will make you happy before the audit.

Have Your Material Ready

Distribute the meeting agenda a day before the meeting and make sure every participant has access to any relevant background material. Participants, of course, have the obligation to review the agenda and background material and arrive at the meeting prepared.

If the team leader or meeting organizer has not provided adequate information about the objectives of the meeting, the participants should take the initiative and ask. No one should arrive at a meeting not knowing why they are there and what is supposed to be accomplished.

Prepare Your Introductory Speech

You need to prepare your introductory speech ahead of time. An introductory speech should be brief and professional and should include an introduction of the customers or auditors who are scheduled to audit the company. Welcome your guests with succinct remarks relating to their position or accomplishments.

It is essential that the auditors are provided with a copy of the executive summary of the company business or the kind of company overview that might be presented by top or senior management. This document can be used as a reference following the meeting.

A hard copy handout of the agenda and presentation will also enable the audience to refer back to points you made in your presentation and view graphics and photos of interest. Additional handouts may include marketing materials, relevant press clippings, and technical documents.

Identify a Facilitator

As mentioned earlier, during the opening meeting you should identify the point person as a liaison to facilitate the auditors. This facilitator will function as the auditors' escort. He or she will act as the coordinator for the audit and will keep a written record of all audit-related activities, address any questions or concerns, find requested documentation, and respond to requests for personnel interviews. Upon request, all your team members should be available to answer questions on subjects of which they have direct knowledge.

In summary, the facilitator's tasks should include the following:

- Confirming that any logistical requirements are available and ready
- Briefly introducing members of the auditee team and their roles
- Allowing auditees to introduce themselves
- Reminding the auditees of the reason and scope for the audit
- Promoting a positive impression
- Noting any observations, findings or requests
- Time keeping
- Confirming communication channels for how the audit will be run and reported
- Escalating any critical items to the team leader and/or the audit authority

Use Your Overview to Show Off Your Company's Achievements

The old adage says that it is what is in the book that matters, not the cover. However, if the cover is not appealing, the book will go unread.

In the case of customer or regulatory audits, that "cover" is provided by the company overview, which is usually in the form of a PowerPoint presentation. Make sure that your "cover" features something significant about your company values and catches the eyes of the auditors. The company overview should give the best impression possible about your management, products and services.

Because customers will seldom sign a non-disclosure or confidentiality agreement prior to your presentation, be sure to include only information that you are willing to share without legal protection.

Time Frame and Format

Keep your formal presentation short and to the point and limit it to no more than 20 minutes. Use the question and answer period following the presentation to provide details and amplification of the points you made during the presentation.

The purpose of the presentation is to guide your audience and to provide emphasis for key points. In preparing the PowerPoint presentation, be careful to adhere to the common principles of effective presentations and ensure that the slides complement your verbal presentation and do not divert the attention of the listener away from your remarks. As a general guideline, you should assume that each slide of your presentation equals 1.0 minute of presentation time.

Content

The ideal presentation should be customized to emphasize the compelling nature of your business. In a standard 20-minute presentation, all of the following elements should be included in your presentation. You will need to determine the order of the presentation and any additional information that should be included.

- Nature of the business: Unique product or technology or business model.
- Management team: Who are the executives? What skills and background do they possess that is relevant? How are decisions made?
- Market: Show the market both qualitatively and quantitatively. What are the market trends? What segment of the market will your company enter? What market migration is planned? How does your value compare with the dominant players? What continuing advantage does your company possess that will enable creation of market share in the target market?
- Intellectual property protection and other barriers to entry: How will the company protect its competitive advantage and discourage others from competing successfully?
- Strategic partners: Which strategic partners have you targeted?
- Marketing and distribution: How does your company market and distribute its products or services?
- Key commercialization milestones: Over the next 5 years, what are the major milestones that the company intends to achieve? How will it get there?
- 5-year financial projection: Present the company's share or stock price and a summary of the company's financial health and projections for the next 5 years.
- Challenges and achievements: Present the last 3 years. What are your major achievement and chal-

lenges? What solutions have you taken to overcome these challenges?

Tips for Creating Powerful Presentations

- The ideal corporate profile should start with background about the company and its corporate history – but keep this to one slide and remember that branding is key. In any presentation, the company's branding *must* be visible. Use graphics and images to keep things interesting and use animation to enliven timelines and milestones.
- The structure of the company – its departments and hierarchies – should be communicated in an easily comprehensible way using illustrations.
- Show global or multi-location operations on a map to help your audience get a clearer picture. You can buy editable maps of various regions.
- Presenting portfolios can be tricky, especially when they are large and diverse. You cannot crowd a single slide with information about all the products your company makes. Instead, use PowerPoint's interactive elements and features to make an attractive portfolio spread over multiple slides. If you need a shortcut, you can purchase a portfolio program available in the market.
- Testimonials from truly happy customers are a good way to demonstrate the value of your products and services.
- You may want to tailor your presentation to your specific auditors.
- At the end of the presentation, be sure to highlight the accolades won from professional bodies and clients.
- Avoid being either overly conservative or optimistic when discussing the future. Be prepared to describe,

quantitatively, the impact if things go better or worse than expected.
- Try closing the presentation with a quote from the Chief Executive Officer (CEO) or the company motto.

Provide Refreshments

If you've been asked to prepare refreshments for the meeting, simplicity is the key to providing foods that can be enjoyed by a variety of people. Consider participants' dietary restrictions, and offer a variety of refreshments that are low-fat, sugar-free, caffeinated and decaffeinated. Depending on the culture, you might consider some of the following suggestions.

Morning refreshments:
- Coffee, with and without caffeine
- Hot water for regular tea and herb tea
- Small donuts and pastries
- Fruit or yoghurt
- Bottled water

Lunch break:
- Most auditors prefer to have lunch within the facility. However, if the auditors agree on eating out, it is best to book the restaurant ahead and pre-define a menu that will suit the time available.

Afternoon refreshments:
- Sodas, diet and regular
- Cookies: offer a variety for different tastes
- Vegetables and dip
- Bottled water
- Coffee, with and without caffeine

The required amount of food depends on the number of people you are serving and the time of day. If you are serving food when people are likely to be hungry (for example, after work or close to a mealtime), allow more per person. The rule of thumb for small appetizers such as cut fruits or vegetables or bits of cookies is 5 to 6 pieces per person. Larger items such as whole fruit, pretzels and yogurt, require as few as 1 piece per person.

Provide plates, napkins, spoons and forks, cups, party picks, serving containers, and other utensils necessary for serving and eating the refreshments. If people have to balance plates on their laps, offer spill-proof, small foods that are easy to handle. Also remember to provide condiments such as creamer, sugar and salt.

Remember to make your guests as comfortable as possible and be prepared for casual questions and discussion about your work or the company during breaks.

Step 7 Summary

The opening meeting represents the first chance to meet the auditors and gives them the opportunity to establish a good audit environment. Here are the elements you must comprehend and do to achieve it;

- The Importance of Starting and Finishing Well
- Tips for Conducting Opening Meetings
- Prepare the Opening Meeting Carefully
- Welcome and Introduce Your Guests
- Make Sure Your Agenda Is Clear
- No Tardiness
- Have Your Material Ready
- Prepare Your Introductory Speech
- Identify a Facilitator

- Use Your Overview to Show Off Your Company's Achievements
- Tips for Creating Powerful Presentations
- Provide Refreshments

Step

8

Remember: It's Showtime!

> *Nothing can stop the man with the right mental attitude from achieving his goal. (Thomas Jefferson)*

Introduction: Don't Forget the Message You Want to Send

Never forget "It's Showtime!" Think about how you want the auditors to remember you and bring all of your style, tone, energy and context with you. Once again, prepare in advance and know what you are going to say. Think along the lines of bullet points in your head. Know what problems you solve, play easy to get, and be ready for anything.

An audit does not assume guilt, but don't let your guard down. If an auditor puts you on the spot, you need to address the query, but you don't have to do so immediately. After all, anything you say could be used against you.

The message that you want to display during an audit is that you have your facility and processes under control and that you know what you are doing.

Understand What the Question Is and Why It Is Asked

Answers to auditors should be clear, complete and based on facts, not speculation or your opinion. Do not be afraid to take a firm stance if the auditor draws an inaccurate conclusion from the material provided. Do not be afraid to SELL the auditor on your response by indicating the value of the action or control you are describing.

Here are some examples:

> *"That is not correct. All of our SMT production team have been trained on soldering techniques and qualified by the authorized institution. The copies of the soldering techniques certificate of each qualified SMT staff are kept by the Human Resource department and available for review anytime should this be considered part of the scope for this audit."*

> or

> *"We have had an active Change Management System in use for two years that records dates, the nature of the changes, the environment and other key fields. During the audit period we expanded the feature set of the system and added authorization and approval fields, which we believe increases the effectiveness of this control."*

When the auditor touches on a data point that you don't clearly understand, ask for immediate clarification by repeating his data point as a question. With this feedback, the auditor will likely expand on his previous statement, which will increase joint understanding of the data point and show the auditor that you are paying close attention.

Certain things that you are accustomed to may be something the auditor rarely sees or hears about. If there is confusion as to what's needed, ask your auditor what objective he is trying to achieve and chances are that your insight into a particular report will provide the information needed to satisfy the request.

Don't Rush

Old people say that every person is considered wise – until he or she opens their mouth. The best attribute you can display during an audit is to listen carefully. Take time to consider what the auditor is asking before you speak.

Practice careful listening by listening for both the content and emotion in the auditor's voice. During a customer audit, listen carefully so you know what challenges your customer needs to resolve.

Leave a little pause after the auditors' words in case they have something to add. Too many listeners take the first chance to rush into speech themselves. Instead, refer back to things said earlier in the conversation to show that you heard correctly.

Always try to answer the auditor with back-up procedures, metrics, data, instructions, policies, and customer satisfaction in your mind. This will eventually help build good sentences and answers that make auditors happy.

Make It Easy

The more helpful and friendly you are, the easier everything will go. Many auditors may not be qualified to test an IT area due to little or no background in IT. Don't be condescending, but do help them try to understand.

A lot of questions that auditors ask are related to variances from year to year. If you know that something has changed significantly, have your answers ready.

If requested, provide the auditor with a comfortable place to work with ample space to organize materials. Keep the room free of non-protocol materials or subject information. Lock any cabinets and drawers in the room.

The facilitator will accompany the auditor at all times during the audit. This may include excursions to the restroom.

Don't Lie

There's no use asking for trouble and that's what a lie will get you. So don't lie. Ever. If you hear your manager misstate something, speak up! The auditors are MUCH more likely to really pound down on you if they find out you lied about something. Their logic is that if you lied about one thing, you have likely lied about others.

Don't Guess

If you aren't sure how to respond to a query, never guess. Instead, find an experienced staff member with expertise in the area you need help with or refer the auditor to alternative personnel. It is all right to say "I am not sure" or "I don't know."

Here are some examples of good responses when you don't know something:

"I am not sure what the frequency or detailed process is, but I have the SOP (standard operating procedure) here. Let me take a look." (Refer to relevant documentation and review it yourself.)

or

"I don't know the correct answer. I believe my supervisor will be able to provide you with an accurate answer or data." (Defer the question to a support person or someone who is more expert in that area.)

If the auditor asks you a question about someone else's job you should answer, "That is not my job" and refer him to the correct person or to your manager to get advice.

Don't Blab or Tell Secrets

Act in response to specific queries only. Stay clear of talking too much, particularly when it is not related to the question. Remember, proper evidence must be ready to support your responses.

Don't let your guard down. Auditors are not your friends. They may try to speak casually to you or make small talk, but do not for a moment let your guard down and never tell someone else's secret. Always remember that the auditors are there to assess your company and your work.

Tips on What Not to Say

There are some statements that may trap you and lead to more audit trails. Below are examples of statements that you should guard against.

Example 1

Auditor: *Have you had difficulty getting prepared for this audit?*

Quality Engineer: *Yes, it took a long time for everyone to close their corrective action requests because people are busy trying to meet their sales targets.*

Auditor's thinking: There are many corrective actions that had to be closed at the last minute. Investigation is needed into the company's commitment and communication on the QMS. I will also need to verify if some errors occurred on the documentations or records.

Example 2

Auditor: *Please tell me about the customer order verification process. Do you have a procedure or work instruction for me to review?*

Sales Order Entry Coordinator: *I am not sure if there is a work instruction for my job. My boss told me what to do and I understood it pretty quickly.*

Auditor's thinking: The ISO standard requires the company to verify the customer order as part of the planning of product realization process. I need to see if there is a work instruction or procedure. If there is, is it available at the employee's work station and does it call for verifying the customer order before entering it into the system? I also need to see the employee competence and training system and records. I need to know the minimum qualification requirement for this position. And I need to check this staff's personnel record to determine what training he/she has received so far.

Example 3

Auditor: *I see that you have several incoming materials that are placed in the 'After Inspection' area. Can you show me the identifications?*

Incoming QC Inspector: *These two materials are to go to inventory, but the other one needs to be sent back to the vendor due to defects found. I have not put the identifications on yet. I don't have time because I need to go home soon, but I remember which is which.*

Auditor's thinking: ISO standard requires all materials and products to be identified. And material that is known to be defective has to be controlled to avoid unintended use. This one is left without identification. This is a non-conformance to the ISO standard.

Example 4

Auditor: *What is the company's quality policy and objective?*

Maintenance Technician: *There is one, but I am not sure what it is. I think we have a copy posted somewhere in the lobby.*

Auditor's thinking: The employee training on the quality system needs to be verified. I will need to review management commitment and communication about the quality management system.

Example 5

Auditor: *Can you tell me your shipping process?*

Shipping Coordinator: *I follow the shipping process correctly as per the work instruction. But there's a lot of work during the month-end and it's really crazy around here. Once in a while I find an order that comes through without a packing slip.*

Auditor's thinking: I will need to see the work instruction and check the procedure to be followed if there is no shipping information.

Example 6

Auditor: *How does your infrastructure support you?*

IT Administrator: *We have problems with our server. There are many cases recorded where the server has been freezing. We have spoken to management, but it is hard for us to get anything done.*

Auditor's thinking: The quality system says management is required to provide sufficient resources. There are questions about management commitment, especially when they know the problem and don't fix it. I need to check the review done during the quality management review meeting, as well as its minutes.

What to Do After an "Oops" Moment

You may at some time mistakenly answer the question the auditors ask. The auditors will usually give you a second chance to clarify or correct your answer. When this happens, be sure to provide clarity or clear up any contradictory statement by referring to more expert staff in the area or to procedures or other documents. If the auditors do not give you a chance to clarify your response, be proactive. Tell the auditor that you would like to make a clarification or correction of what you said earlier. Make sure the auditor notes the correction.

Take Notes

Concisely list and tie together the main points covered in a session. This will confirm that the auditor has been listening to you. The auditor may not state everything required, but he or she may state specific experiences. Be attentive and learn.

How to Deal with Dead Air

Sometimes in an interview situation there may be a gap in the conversation – dead air. The auditor may be pausing to review the notes or read the documents – or he may be hoping that you will say more.

Human nature says that we need to fill in this dead air with talk, but that is not always the best thing to do. Dead air is normal and you do not need to fill it with any information that may cause the auditor to ask you more questions. The best thing to do is to be silent and wait until the auditors ask the next question.

Remember: The Less Said the Better

Most auditors will apply open-ended questions which require you to elaborate and stimulate the conversation instead of answering yes or no. Answer all questions as directly as possible, but don't add any unnecessary information. And remember, think before you speak.

Be Aware of Body Language

Knowing how to read nonverbal signals can be an invaluable asset in interview situations. When auditors need to determine that the data they are working with are accurate, they can usually rely on objective tests. However, in interpersonal interactions, on-the-spot decisions must frequently be made with little opportunity for immediate objective verification.

Be conscious of both the auditors' and your own body language. From the moment you walk in the door or meet people, your body is busy telling people all about you. Your body can tell people that you are confident with your system.

Don't Add Information

Do not volunteer any information to the auditor. The auditor will have a lot of questions for you and many specific requests. There is no need to volunteer any more information than you need to since you never know how that information may be used against you. It is best to stay quiet and only answer the specific questions asked and only hand over records specifically requested. Do not make additional conversation and do not get drawn into what may only seem to be harmless chit chat with the auditor.

Answer all questions briefly, honestly and accurately. Do not elaborate on a question unless questioned further for detail. When appropriate, limit responses to yes or no answers. Only answer questions on subjects of which you have direct knowledge. Be confident that your response is accurate and factual and be prepared to supply supporting documentation.

Wait and Be Silent

During the audit, keep quiet until you are required to speak. Your objective is simply to get in and out as quickly as possible. Even when the information you offer is harmless, it may cause the auditor to journey down another byway.

When in doubt, remain silent. If you're in doubt about answering a specific question or handing over some information because you fear that it could be improper, then consult your manager immediately. It is better to take note of the question or request and let the auditor know that you will get back to him or her with the reply shortly.

It is a good idea to have a standard reply ready for such questions: "I am going to take note of the specific question you are asking me, just to make sure I understand it correctly, and I will get back to you shortly with the answer."

If the auditor insists on getting a reply right away, simply restate what you have said with a little variation: "I understand that you would like to get your work done quickly, and believe me I want you to get it done as quickly as possible too, so I will take note of your question and get back to you just as soon as I possibly can."

If they keep insisting, keep repeating your answer. The auditor will realize sooner or later that you will not budge from your position. Afterwards, call your manager or an expert in that area immediately to find out what potential risks there are in answering the question or handing over the specific information to the auditor.

Express Your Thanks

When the audit is done, you or the host of the audited area should thank the auditor for his great and/or thorough job. Don't just say 'great job', but describe what you are recognizing in specific, tangible terms. Emphasize the impact on you, your team, and the company so the auditor can see the positive consequences of his/her work.

Step 8 Summary

Remember: It's Showtime! Here are what most important factors to adhere to;

- Don't Forget the Message You Want to Send
- Understand What the Question Is and Why It Is Asked
- Don't Rush
- Make It Easy
- Don't Lie
- Don't Guess
- Don't Blab or Tell Secrets
- Tips on What Not to Say
- What To Do After an "Oops" Moment
- Take Notes
- How to Deal with Dead Air
- Remember: The Less Said the Better
- Be Aware of Body Language
- Don't Add Information
- Wait and Be Silent
- Express Your Thanks

Step

9

Give Them Only What They Want

> *Think twice before you speak, because your words and influence will plant the seed of either success or failure in the mind of another.*
> *(Napoleon Hill)*

Introduction: Find Out What the Auditors Want

During communications on planning and scheduling the audit, the external auditor will send you a meeting request and at the same time may send you a list of questions or bullet points to be covered. This will form the basis of the documentation you will need to collect.

Come to the meeting prepared with documentation that supports your compliance of the control objectives or shows progress in mitigating already identified issues.

This documentation may include policies and procedures, change management logs, audit check sheets or logs, printouts of user permissions and computer configuration settings, etc.

Remember that you may ask for clarification of any audit item at any time, even before the scheduled meeting.

TIP: Auditors are not going to ask for items that they don't actually need. They understand and appreciate that you are busy not only helping them, but also doing your regular tasks. Wasting your time is not something they want to do.

Choose Your Representatives Carefully

Select people in the company and task them to speak with the auditors according to the applicable standard. The people you select should be optimist, and believe that they have a great system and are highly appreciated by the management.

The scope of the audit will give you tips on selecting the people who should be involved:

- Executives: overviews of the entire organization, leadership commitment
- Managers: details about policies, procedures, internal controls, general workings of their areas
- Supervisors: detailed information about day-to-day operations
- Employees: detailed information about day-to-day operations in specific areas
- Others: contractors, vendors, and appropriate personnel from adjacent systems

  TIP: It is all right for your representatives to talk about their successes as long as they can present some proofs.

Supply All Requested Documents but Don't Hand Over All Records

In your effort to be cooperative, you might be tempted to hand over all your records. Avoid doing this. Don't bring any documents that were not specifically requested.

It is best to get the auditor to put a list of what he or she wants in writing. Then make copies of the requested documents and hand them over before the end of the audit. Make a second copy for the record of items provided to the auditor.

You should not allow auditors to retrieve documents/materials themselves.

Don't Volunteer Information

Auditors are not supposed to be on an open-ended hunt, but anything you pass along can open the door to other questions. So don't volunteer information. The auditor can always ask for more, but there is no reason to offer more than is requested.

If you feel the auditor has overlooked or given short shrift to relevant material, by all means provide it and ask if it modifies his decision. This is a very important exception to the earlier tip on volunteering no information until it is requested.

Organize Your Records

It is your duty to keep and maintain the records that prove your quality requirements and standards. Keeping those records in an organized format lends credibility to you as a good manager.

Auditors can go back years from the date you produced a report, so be sure you keep proper files. Disorganized or incomplete records can cause an auditor to assume you have either made a mistake or are hiding something and attempting to make it hard for the auditor to find it. This will only encourage the auditor to work even harder to find an error or omission in your system.

There are excellent records and documents management software programs that can help you keep records electronically. But a simple accordion folder with multiple sub-folders is sufficient to keep sorted records in one place.

> **TIP:** Ideally, records should be separated by year or product/service and divided into main categories.

Address Auditor Observations

During the audit, it is likely the auditor will make "observations" relating to the conduct of the process, system, documentation, etc. The facilitator should work with the host team to make every effort to address and correct these observations while the audit is taking place.

If non-conformances are observed during the audit, you may decide to immediately correct issues that do not need an investigation of root causes. By demonstrating the effectiveness of your procedures for handling such issues, you may impress the auditors. You can also ask the auditors to acknowledge such actions in their final audit report.

When corrective actions to address a non-conformance require expert root cause investigation, it is best to leave this until after the audit and then follow your established corrective action process. A full response to the auditors about the issue should include the investigation of root causes and the implementation of measures to prevent reoccurrence. Otherwise, you may create an impression that it is acceptable to do patch-up work and this will not be viewed favourably.

Again, auditors will be impressed to see your proactive actions and implementation of changes early.

Keep Track of All Documentation

Keep track of all communication with the auditors and all documentation provided to them. If there is a document you were not able to track down, don't disclose the fact. Often, records that were requested won't be needed based on the quality of other information you provide.

Give Only Copies of Documents

Auditors are authorized to review the originals of all supporting documents, but never give up those originals. Make copies of all the records the auditors ask for and keep all of the originals. Do not assume that the auditor will care for your records in the same way you would. If records get lost or misplaced, you will be held responsible for those missing records.

During the audit, ensure that all photocopies provided to the auditor for review are marked as 'uncontrolled' or 'commercial in confidence' as necessary, and provide the correct version.

If you are ever in a situation where you are forced to give the originals to auditors, the auditors should give you a receipt for what they are taking. Make sure the list is comprehensive so there is no dispute later on, and make copies of those documents before handing them over to the auditors.

Step 9 Summary

To form the basis of the documentation you will need to collect, follow these essential steps;

- Find Out What the Auditors Want
- Choose Your Representatives Carefully
- Supply All Requested Documents But Don't Hand Over All Records
- Don't Volunteer Information
- Organize Your Records
- Address Auditor Observations
- Keep Track of All Documentation
- Give Only Copies of Documents

Step

10

Be Cool

> It is a great thing to know the season for speech and the season for silence. (Seneca)

Introduction: Use Your Interpersonal Skills

You are scheduled to meet with an auditor over a topic that you're a subject matter expert on. But how do you handle yourself in the audit and come out smelling like a rose and not do yourself more harm than good? Your interpersonal skills during the interview will contribute to the quality and success of the audit.

Effective interpersonal skills will also help build co-operative relationships. The following tips may be used in any audit situation and should be made known to your entire audit team.

Project Confidence

The single most important element in being the kind of person everyone wants to talk with is...confidence. Your attitude about yourself bounces from you to other people. When you show you are happy and confident, the auditor will be happy to see you – and will have confidence in you, too.

What should you do if you are not confident? The magic answer is to "act as if". Act as if you *are* brave and confident. Assume that others are happy to see you. You've got to believe – or at least act as though you believe – that the auditor is going to enjoy spending a few minutes with you.

It might feel artificial at first, but the more you "act as if", the more the new behaviours will begin to feel comfortable. Feel free to think, "Help! I don't know what to say! I'm afraid I'm going to spill something!" Think anything you like, but stand up straight, smile, shake hands, and calmly and charmingly say, "It's a pleasure to meet you." This will show that you are confident.

Maintain Good Business Posture

With any luck, you already have good posture. If your posture needs work, work on it before and after, not during, the audit. The person who stands tall but not stiffly, and moves in a calm and purposeful way commands respect.

Maintaining a confident business posture and good eye contact during the interview is important. Confident posture includes the way you hold your head. In general, keep your head level. A level head indicates an assured, candid, and capable nature. It might also give your voice fuller tones and make you seem to be looking people straight in the eye.

A bowed head, staring off into space, eyes studying the floor or avoiding an auditor's gaze makes you look unsure and vulnerable. It may be interpreted as disinterest or, even worse, dishonesty.

Listen Actively

Listen patiently to what the auditors have to say and the questions that they ask, even if you believe their points are wrong or irrelevant. Indicate acceptance – not necessarily agreement – by nodding or perhaps injecting an occasional "I understand" or "I see."

After you are asked a question, restate the auditor's points and/or questions briefly and accurately. Think of yourself as a mirror. Encourage the auditor to expand upon his or her points or questions. Occasionally make summary responses to display your understanding of the discussion. For example, "The audit will encompass only the ERP system" or "The key control in this audit is user permissions."

While making these summary statements, keep your tone neutral and try not to lead the auditor to incorrect assumptions or conclusions about the information shared.

Control disruptions from cell phones, pagers and text messages. Focus on the auditor and don't allow yourself to be distracted by what is going on around you or by your own thoughts and concerns. Let the auditor talk first and actively listen to what he has to say.

Remember, it is hard to listen with your mouth open.
Avoid looking at your watch during the audit. This can be a very insulting gesture. It suggests that you are trying to gauge whether you think what the auditor is saying is worth your time. Let the facilitator take care of the schedule and be the timekeeper.

Be Cooperative

Try to establish a feeling that you are on the same wavelength with the auditor. We tend to feel warm toward people who agree with us. Use the words "we", "our", "ourselves" and "us" to establish a sense of kinship and belonging.

It is important for you set a positive environment for the audit. Use a conversational style during the interview, maintain a positive attitude, avoid being defensive, and give clear and concise answers to the auditor.

When you feel you've answered the question, move on and don't ramble or keep repeating yourself.

Allow auditors to question any staff member (i.e. do not steer the auditor away). However, if the auditor chooses to speak to your staff, watch to see if your staff has difficulty answering questions. In that case, you may want to ask the auditor if you could help to rephrase the question, direct the conversation, or make clarifications so your staff clearly understand.

Always deliver something you have promised and never cause a deliberate delay. If for some reason you cannot deliver a copy of a document quickly, explain the reason for delay. Take a note and try to provide the document before finishing the audit.

> **TIP:** It is not unusual for an auditee to feel nervous during an interview. A good auditor will try to make the auditee feel at ease to improve communication.

Remain Cordial

Set the proper tone. Be available and maintain a professional, polite, cordial and cooperative demeanour at all times. Yes, you are likely feeling stressed out about the whole ordeal and perhaps are frustrated or even angry that you were chosen to be audited. However, taking it out on the auditor will get you absolutely nowhere.

Auditors are human. If you are cordial with them, they will likely be civil with you. This is not just a matter of manners; remember, auditors can exercise some discretion when it comes to reducing and assessing the findings.

Behaving civilly will definitely not work against you, but rude or outright abusive behaviour will. This in no way means that you need to be friends with the auditor and take him out for a cup of coffee afterwards, but you could consider offering him a cup of coffee and a muffin during the break. Strive to make a good impression throughout the audit.

Stay On Scope

Staying on scope is critical to having a successful audit interview. Remember these points:

- Listen to the question carefully.
- Use active listening to clarify the question.
- Form a clear, complete and factual answer.
- Do not elaborate on data, expand on points, or go off on semi-related tangents.
- Stay within the defined scope of the audit agenda that you were sent before the meeting.
- Do not be afraid to pull the auditor back into scope should he or she drift.

Most audits find their graceful, convenient, and natural end when those involved realize it is time to end. In the event that you are trapped by a long-winded auditor, signalling wildly or rolling your eyes to the facilitator is unacceptable.

What should you do? Try a phrase like one of these:

"I have been monopolizing you. I am sure you want to talk with other people here."

"I should not keep you. I know there are other people who want to talk with you."

"I think I am getting the signal from the facilitator that it's time to move on to the next person on the schedule."

Don't Argue

Arguing, changing the subject and losing your temper should be avoided during the audit.

Every auditor should give you a chance to formally write a response to any findings. If you disagree with something, do explain it to the auditor (and back it up with evidence) but don't argue. If they still don't understand, just say "I will document it and send my formal response."

Never take up a fight with the auditor. Your organization is distributing cash for the auditor to do his or her work and you are actually their client. Remember, the auditor can't send you to prison or have you fired. The auditor is there only to verify and assure that the QMS meets the necessities of the standard.

Don't Take It Personally

Do not get emotionally involved in the auditor's questions or your answers. Stay calm, cool and collected. If you are unable to answer any of the auditor's questions, don't be afraid to ask for a temporary deference so that you can do the proper research and contact the auditor in a timely manner with your response.

> **TIP:** The whole goal of an audit is to make things better and to protect people's data. They are not "out to get you". Don't take it personally.

Smile

With all the above advice, you might be wondering what physical movements are left to you. The smile will work miracles. It is the most important body language of all, signalling that you are cordial, comfortable in your skin, and receptive to whatever the other person might say.

The tendency of the human being is to reflect the emotion the other person displays. If you smile, chances are very good the auditor will smile back, the conversation will go smoothly and the audit interview will end nicely.

Step 10 Summary

You will need to use this basic attitude to make the audit enjoyable;

- Use Your Interpersonal Skills
- Project Confidence
- Maintain Good Business Posture
- Listen Actively
- Be Cooperative
- Remain Cordial
- Stay On Scope
- Don't Argue
- Don't Take It Personally
- Smile

Step

11

Know Your Right to Fight

> *The best victory is when the opponent surrenders of its own accord before there are any actual hostilities... It is best to win without fighting. (Sun-tzu)*

Introduction: You Don't Have to Accept All Findings

Do not be afraid to appeal the results of an audit. If you believe that the audit was done unfairly or the auditor made a mistake in his or her assessment, then speak with the auditor to try to reach a compromise. If this doesn't help, escalate the issue to your upper management and – with their approval – speak with the auditor's manager. Then go through whatever appeals process is available.

If you are involved in an ISO audit, the auditors will provide a presentation about their organization during the opening meeting. This will include the audit purpose, methodology and schedule. At the same time, they will explain your right to appeal should you not agree with their audit findings and observations.

If you are being audited for a standard other than ISO, you may want to check if there is any similar process of appeal.

Knowing your appeal rights from the outset will give you comfort that there is an appropriate system or process in place should you need it.

Seek Clarification

Sometimes the items you provide the auditor might not be exactly what the auditor is looking for due to differences in terminology or the fact that your auditor may be trying to target a specific population or procedure. This is not anyone's fault, but it might explain why something still appears on the open items list. Don't ever be afraid to seek clarification of the auditor's observations or findings. For example:

- **Ask for more evidence**
  Pick a concern and ask the auditors to evaluate it further and collect more information to support their concern.

- **Ask for help**
  Shift the auditors from "audit" to "consult" mode. Request that they examine a specific area that you "need help in."

- **Ask for more discussion**
  Ask for more debriefings and meetings between the auditors and your personnel to discuss the auditors' concerns. Keep asking for explanations and for more and more background information.

Know the Findings That You Should Not Accept

The final results of an audit – the findings – may not truly represent the concerns that were identified during the audit.

There are several types of findings that you should not accept. They are:

- **Oral findings**
  Never accept an oral report as the final result of an audit. An oral finding is an opinion only.

- **Findings without standards**
  A finding that is not based upon the official standards of the audit in some manner is a finding that falls outside the scope of the audit and the auditing organization's authority. Never accept this type of finding from a regulatory agency.

- **Summary findings**
  Don't accept two findings for the same problem.

- **Findings based on findings**
  Auditors who get tied up reviewing previous audits will often make findings based on other findings. However, the situation has probably changed since the previous audit, and the findings that the auditor reviewed may or may not be valid at the time of the current audit. Do not accept such findings unless you confirm they are valid for the current situation.

- **Disguised recommendations**
  When auditors would like to see improvements, they may make a finding without defining the problem. Unless the auditor can explain why an improvement is needed, you should not accept the finding. You may want to do what the auditor is recommending, but you don't want it to show up as a failure.

- **Hearsay findings**
  Do not accept a finding that is based on what the auditor was told by a party who is not involved in the audit.

- **Out of proportion findings**
  Do not accept a finding where the auditors get carried away with themselves and blow a problem out of proportion. For example, if one person is caught not wearing proper production clothes, that does not mean that the facility's protocol is poor.

- **Irrelevant findings**
  Other than the specific documents required by the standard, if an auditor complains that you have no formal procedure for his review, yet this particular facility has a proven record of high positive ratings from customers, then the finding is irrelevant.

Know When to Escalate

Situations where you may need to escalate an audit issue include:

- **Poor criteria**
  If an auditor didn't apply good criteria during the audit, a minor finding may be considered critical. Try to convince him that, based on the standard, the finding was minor. If the auditor does not want to listen, the issue needs to be escalated to management. The exit meeting will provide you with another opportunity to clarify and provide objective evidence to support your defence. However, if the auditor keeps his position and submits his report that way, your company has a right to appeal to the auditor's company or registrar body and may decide to switch to another auditor or audit company.

- **Lack of objectivity**
  At some point in an audit, you may be faced with the unhappy realization that an auditor will not be objec-

tive in his evaluation of your program, either because of his own personality and experience, his bad attitude, or because the two of you cannot get along. At this point, escalation to management is strongly recommended, for bad auditors can seriously affect the reputation of your company. Report the auditor's poor attitude and lack of objectivity to both your management and his. This won't prevent any inaccurate findings, but it will minimize the impact on your company. Elevate the conflict to your management and let your management settle the differences with his management strategically.

Step 11 Summary

It is very important that you know your right when you believe that the audit was done unfairly. Here is what you should do;

- You Don't Have to Accept All Findings
- Seek Clarification
- Know the Findings That You Should Not Accept
- Know When to Escalate

Step

12

Conduct a Memorable
Exit Meeting and Audit Closing

> *A satisfied customer is the best business strategy of all.*
> *(Michael LeBoeuf)*

Introduction: Final Impressions Are Important

The closing, final or exit meeting represents the final chance for the auditing team to display its professionalism, as well as an opportunity to maintain a positive relationship with your auditors.

Auditors usually hold individual pre-exit meetings at the end of each field audit. That means there should be no surprises during the exit meeting, and all issues should be resolved before the meeting begins. To ensure that the final meeting runs smoothly, auditors may need to conduct a series of pre-exit meetings to tie up any loose ends. Then, the "real" exit meeting, which is often attended by senior managers who did not directly participate in the audit, can be confined to a presentation and discussion of the audit process and results, rather than serving as a working meeting.

A well-run closing meeting draws the audit to a close in a professional and controlled manner.

Conduct a Pre-Exit Meeting

As the team leader, you should have the auditors present their preliminary findings in a pre-exit meeting with you whenever possible. This meeting will occur either at the end of the audit or shortly thereafter.

The pre-exit meeting is very important to get a sense of the auditors' satisfaction and to pre-discuss and obtain a detailed understanding of any issues. Having an early agreement with auditors increases the chance of a positive audit result.

Encourage the auditors to ignore what they may have written so far and instead to discuss each of their concerns in plain language. By getting the auditors to open up and thoroughly discuss each concern, both you and they will learn more about the actual problems that have been found. Avoid arguments in this meeting. Instead, ensure that you understand what it is the auditors are trying to say.

If you have made appropriate changes and improvements in your program, you must describe the changes with evidence and request the auditors to reconsider the findings.

The auditors will arrive with a prepared text (which they may or may not give you at the end of the audit), and they will not deviate from the text unless directly questioned. The auditors will have sandbagged their positions and have prepared long lists of supporting evidence for each of their findings, which they will use if questioned. The best approach to use in these pre-exit meetings is to break down the formality and request the auditors to discuss their findings in their own words. You can do this by asking after each finding is presented: "How serious a problem is this?" "What are the consequences if we don't take action on this?"

Don't be afraid to have the auditors resort to their "hit lists". Remember, you want to hear what they have to say. Usually the supporting evidence does a better job of explaining the findings and their significance than the findings themselves. If the findings are valid, the discussion will help you to better understand the problems involved. If the findings are not valid, the auditors will have a difficult time discussing them, and chances are that they will not report them to your management.

Once you are both in agreement, the exit meeting is ready to be conducted.

Know the Function of the Exit Meeting

Sometimes an exit meeting is not so much a debriefing as it is a formal presentation of the results of the audit. This formal presentation is required in order to ensure that your upper management is present at the exit meeting, including possibly the Chief Executive Officer.

The formal presentation is critical because once it has been conducted your management has, in essence, placed a stamp of approval on the audit findings. In a formal presentation, you will want to be sure that you and your management are clear on the significance of the auditors' findings.

Interactions during the closing meeting should take place primarily between the management, the facilitator and the auditor. Other members of the team should not attempt to contribute to the proceedings unless invited to do so.

Select the Right Participants for the Meeting

Those who will have responsibility for carrying out a decision should be represented in the decision-making process. When the responsible party is not at the meeting, he or she has no opportunity to contribute to the solution or commit to its terms. Imposing a decision without consultation often results in resentment, doubt, and failure.

Before selecting participants, ask yourself the following:

- Who is involved with this subject?
- Whose authority do we need?
- Who will be interested?
- Who can help with this problem?
- Who has or needs information on this problem?

The following people should generally be invited to the exit meeting:

- Top management representative
- Quality representative
- Department heads
- Functional managers, especially those functions where the findings were identified
- Some key functional staff

If your meeting is likely to hang up on a key point, you may need someone with the authority to authorize decisions. For example, if a proposal is likely to stretch the limits of company policy, you may need someone who can authorize an exception. It's very difficult to proceed with creative problem-solving when all involved know their suggestions may be made futile by a ruling from higher up.

Be sure that everyone included in your meeting is concerned with its outcome. It often seems natural to include a whole group; however, on closer examination you may realize that several individuals have no interest in the outcome of the meeting and will contribute nothing to its success. They will be grateful if you don't involve them in the exit meeting and allow them to continue with more useful work.

If you sense that leaving some people out would risk offending them, allow them to choose for themselves. Explain the purpose of the meeting and why you don't think their attendance is necessary and then let them decide for themselves whether or not to attend. They'll appreciate both your respect for their time and the consideration you've shown by keeping them informed.

Inform the Meeting Participants

Participants need to be informed about your meeting well in advance. Be sure that the time, location and purpose are made clear. Also establish a firm time at which the meeting is scheduled to end. The tone, the wording and the method you use to announce your meeting can affect the attitudes participants bring to it. They can be informed by memo, by telephone or in a personal conversation. But whenever possible, the invitation should be official.

You may want to call or invite the participants personally. Consider a personal invitation for the boss; for example, "Say, we'll be going over this at a meeting at 3 pm today. I'd appreciate it if you would come in and help." That way, he or she will come in expecting to contribute to the meeting.

Whether the invitation was made personally or not, always provide some written notification that will serve as a reminder to all participants. Often, the announcement need include only a statement of the purpose of the meeting, the date, schedule, and location. However, giving additional details may encourage participants to contribute much more productively. For example, if they have reports or data available that might be useful, participants should be requested to bring them. If they will be expected to make spoken reports, they should be given time to prepare. If you will be attempting to solve a specific problem, they should be given an opportunity to think about the problem and begin formulating solutions and contingencies in advance.

Be sure to provide participants with the single most important piece of information – a concise statement of the purpose of the meeting.

Start and End On Time

Be sure the exit meeting is conducted on schedule. If it is not, pre-alert management or the key people who will be involved in the meeting.

Start the meeting on time and end it on time (or even early). Starting on time requires discipline from you as the chairperson and from the participants. Arriving late shows a lack of consideration for all those who were on time. If all participants know that the chairperson is going to start the meeting right on time, there is a much greater likelihood that everyone else will make the effort to be punctual.

Let the Auditor Talk First

At the closing meeting, the lead auditor will give an overview of the audit and its outcome. You will be presented with the summary of the auditors' observations (good and bad) and a list of issues, if any. The list of issues is very likely to be listed as findings in the audit report.

The facilitator should attend the closing meeting to compare the deficiencies presented by the lead auditor to those recorded during the audit and discuss any discrepancies.

Remember the No Surprises Rule

There will be some time allocated by the lead auditor to further clarify the issues noted during the audit, but most of these issues should have been discussed and accepted or otherwise at the time they were observed and noted. If it is related to the management, be sure you have informed them prior to the meeting. Do not leave important issues until the closing meeting, for there may not be sufficient time to discuss them.

Suggest Counter Measures and Improvements

Politely request clarification from the auditor of all observations addressed and/or items that were corrected during the audit. If any of the observations noted deal with not meeting requirements, carefully point out your interpretation of the requirements and then explain your intentions for improvement.

If you can clearly identify an appropriate corrective action in response to an observation, indicate what measures you plan to take to correct the observation immediately. However, you should not commit to a future action that you do not intend to make or are unable to fulfill.

Wrap Up with a Clear Statement

Wrap up the meeting with a clear statement of the next steps and who is to take them. If any decisions were made at the meeting (even if the decision was to "study the issue more"), you should clearly summarize what needs to be done and who is going to do it. If the organizer fails to do this, one of the participants needs to speak up and request clarification of the next steps. This is crucial. If the participants leave the meeting and no one is accountable for taking action on the decisions that were made, then the meeting will have been a waste of everyone's time.

To put things in their proper perspective at the end of the auditors' presentation, ask the auditors to give an overall rating of your program. If their response does not match what they have said about the significance of the findings, ask the auditors "How can these findings all be serious problems when you say I have an excellent program overall?"

Keep Records

Regardless of the style of the exit meeting, you will want to have a record of the meeting to refer to in the future. If you need to, tape-record the meeting or have a stenographer present. Give a copy of the tape or the transcript to the auditors. You may never listen to the tape or refer to the transcript again, but their existence will keep the auditors honest.

Express Your Appreciation

The single most effective characteristic you can bring into this meeting is the ability to show appreciation no matter how the audit went. What will make you stand out and be remembered later are the pleasant remarks that show your genuine pleasure at something the auditor and other people say, do, or have done.

An effective appreciation is brief, sincere, specific, and makes the auditor or other staff feel important. If you have found something the auditor or other staff is proud of and mention it during the exit meeting, they will go away thinking nice thoughts about themselves ... and you.

Say Good-Bye

You will want to say good-bye to each auditor individually. Walk them outside your doorway upon their departure. Take leave of your hosts with a brief, sincere, "Thank you once again for auditing us and suggesting future improvements. I look forward to meeting you again in the future."

Respond to the Audit in Writing

It is important to be co-operative and to commit to providing a written response to the audit findings. If critical non-conformances were noted during the audit and the auditors are likely to request a product recall or present a report that may result in a request to vary or suspend your licence, you should start working on your response immediately and be prepared to present it to the auditor in person.

As the audit team leader, you are the company's contact for receiving the audit report and answering any follow-up questions that the auditors may have after leaving the site. You may delegate the responsibility for coordinating any corrective actions and compiling the audit report, but you should be the one to conduct final verification before submitting the report to the auditor.

See the sample of the corrective action report at the Appendix and visit my website www.winningtheaudit.com to explore the type of report that fits to your requirements.

Conduct a Post-Audit Review

A post-audit review should be conducted to address any areas of weakness identified by your personnel during the audit and not detected by the auditors. It is better to correct these weaknesses now rather than wait for the auditors to identify them the next time around.

Hold the post-audit meeting with your personnel within a week after the results of the audit are in. Thank them for tolerating the auditors and compliment them on their performance where warranted.

During the meeting:

- Go over the results of the audit in detail, adding your interpretation of the significance of each finding to your overall program.
- Discuss what actions will be taken in the near and long term as a result of the findings and recommendations of the auditors. Ask for suggestions on how to do a better job of handling the next audit.
- Cross reference action item status reports to the audit records, so that both you and future auditors can verify what has and has not been closed out from a previous audit.
- Prepare your own list of audit action items and factor these into your normal planning process. Track the action items and prepare status reports, especially for the audit items.

Be Sure to Follow Up

If the auditors have requested a written response to the findings, do so within the timeline provided. About one to three months after the audit, you may call the auditors and discuss what you have done as a result of their audit.

If you can, compliment them on those parts of the audit that you feel were of the most value to you. The auditors will appreciate your compliments and this will make the next audit run smoother.

Celebrate Your Success

Celebrate your achievements and team successes publicly. Reward and recognize teamwork and high performers. You may make some aspect of compensation, such as bonuses or tokens, linked to audit results (depending on corporate practices).

See the sample of the external quality audit result communication email at the Appendix and visit my website www.winningtheaudit.com to explore the type of communication that fits to your requirements.

Every achievement that indicates a win for a team member should be publicly recognized throughout the company.

Don't forget, people need to know that their efforts for the company are recognized and appreciated. After all, you can't be proud of yourself until somebody else has been proud of you.

Step 12 Summary

Finally, to create a memorable exit meeting and audit closing, as well as an opportunity to make the next audit run smoother, below are the crucial steps for you to follow;

- Final Impressions Are Important
- Conduct a Pre-Exit Meeting
- Know the Function of the Exit Meeting
- Select the Right Participants for the Meeting
- Inform the Meeting Participants
- Start and End On Time
- Let the Auditor Talk First
- Remember the No Surprises Rule
- Suggest Counter Measures and Improvements
- Wrap Up with a Clear Statement
- Keep Records
- Express Your Appreciation
- Say Good-Bye
- Respond to the Audit in Writing
- Conduct a Post-Audit Review
- Be Sure to Follow Up
- Celebrate Your Success

Appendix

Appendix 1 – Sample of External Quality Audit Communication

Good Morning Everyone,

We are pleased to advise you that we have received the detail schedule of the (ISO 9001 Recertification) or (Customer Name) Audit. A calendar of activities and audit plan were confirmed and established with (the auditing company name) that the audit will be conducted as follows:

Month, Date, Year   : Company location #1
Month, Date, Year   : Company location #2
Month, Date, Year   : Company location #3

The audit teams were identified based on the audit plan, requirement set by (the auditing company name), and the direction by the head of departments. Enclosed please find the audit plan for each location and familiarize yourself with items/processes to be audited and prepare for a successful audit. Please let (name) know if the auditee names are not appropriate.

Individual time slot/meeting invitation will be sent to all auditees. However the auditor has the right to change the time based on his/her observations and progress. Please make the necessary adjustments to your schedule to accommodate the audit plan.

The auditor will be looking for evidence of effective implementation of all controlled QMS document. Everyone must use only the latest approved and controlled QMS documents listed (application system used). Auditees will need to review all documents that pertain to their job responsibilities and know the related QMS documents. If your procedure(s) do not reflect your current processes, please have them updated accordingly prior to the audit.

As housekeeping is part of observations, please ensure that your respective areas are orderly and clean. If you are not listed as the auditee, it does not mean you are excluded. It's key for everyone to be prepared in their respective areas. The auditor may, at random, decide to speak with you.

Should you require assistance on the QMS documentation, or have any questions relating to this communication, please don't hesitate to contact the Quality Management at your earliest convenience. Your continued support in helping us maintain our high standard is appreciated.

Let's work together for the success of the (ISO 9001 Recertification) or (Customer) Audit.

Thank you.

Regards,
(Name)

Appendix 2 – Sample of Internal Quality Audit Communication

Good Morning Everyone,

In compliant with ISO 9001:2008 Quality Management System, we are pleased to advise that the Internal Quality Audit Schedule will be as follows:

(Company location #1):   Month, Date, Year
(Company location #2):   Month, Date, Year

Attached please find our detail Internal Audit calendar and activities for your review. Individual time slot/meeting invitation will be sent to all Auditees. Please make the necessary adjustments to your schedule to accommodate the internal audit plan and contact (Name) immediately if you are not available at that time and propose the new schedule.

One area the auditors will be looking at is the progress and implementation against audit findings from last year and recent audits. Quality Management department will soon begin closely following up on any outstanding items with the process owners and make necessary meeting/discussion/preparation to ensure its appropriate closure.

The accomplishment of Internal Quality Audit is the critical milestone in order to maintain our ISO 9001:2008 certificate.

Should you require assistance on the QMS documentation, or have any questions relating to this communication, please don't hesitate to contact your manager or Quality Management department at your earliest convenience. Your continued support in helping us accomplishing this critical milestone is appreciated.

Thank you.

Regards,
(Name)
(Title)

Appendix 3 – Sample of External Quality Audit Result Communication

Hello Everyone,

On Month, Date, Year our company was undergone the (Customer Name) audit. The (Customer Name) is based out of Europe, well known within the (type of industry), and have been our loyal customer for (number) years. As such (Customer Name) is an important organization in our (division) business.

The auditors looked for evidence of effective implementation of our Quality Management System in order to maintain the certification for (Product Name) series and we have successfully passed the audit. A total of (number) employees were audited. The auditors were very satisfied with the effective implementation of our quality management system and the continual improvement taken.

During the closing meeting, the auditors mentioned that we have an excellent quality management system implementation. Additionally we noted their satisfaction when auditing the (areas or processes). Production looks well organized. Work instructions were readily available for reference during assembly. Product / process identification and segregation were good.

During the audit, the auditors have identified (number) minor nonconformity and (number) opportunity for improvement. They are listed as follows;

Minor nonconformity:
- (Brief explanation on the finding)

Opportunity for improvement:
- (Brief explanation on the finding)

The auditors have indicated they do not foresee any issues that may impair our existing (Product Name) certification. The Quality team will be working closely with all respective process owners to effectively close-out all pending items.

I would like to take this opportunity to thank all auditees and everyone in the team who has directly or indirectly participated during this audit and making the (Customer Name) Audit a success. Your outstanding cooperation and commitment has displayed strong teamwork!

What's Next:

With all the exhaustive work and effort our teams have applied to accomplish this milestone, we appreciate the continued support of all employees to maintain this high standard.

Well done Team!

Thank you and best regards,
(Name)
(Title)

Appendix 4 – Sample of Internal Quality Audit Plan

COMPANY LOGO	Internal Quality Audit Plan	Form-02 Quality Management Version XX DD/MM/YYYY

Audit Sites	
Dates	
Scope	
Standards	
No of Shift	
Languages	
Audit Team	Leader: Member:

Time	Audit Item	Auditees	Auditors
9:00 – 9:30	**1. OPENING MEETING**		
9:30 – 10:30	**2. HUMAN RESOURCES** • Competence, Awareness & Training • Job Descriptions • Training Needs & Analysis • Performance Review Process • Training Record & Matrix • Responsibility, Authority, Communication • Organization Chart		
10:30 – 12:00	**3. BUSINESS DEV.** • Business Overview • Customer Engagement & Contract Review • Customer Satisfaction, • Management Review • Product End-of-Life Planning and Communication • Sales & Forecast • Handling Customer Order • Customer Service • Handling Customer Feedback/Complaint • Handling Customer Property		
12.00 – 12.30	Lunch Break		
13:00 – 14:30	**4. INCOMING AND INVENTORY** • Receiving • Purchased Product Verification • Inventory Management, • Preservation of Product, • Identification & Traceability, • Control of Nonconforming Product		
14:30 – 16:00	**5. ENGINEERING** • Design and Development, • Internal, Customer, and Regulatory Requirements • Verification, Validation, and Approval • Internal and External Communication • Product Configuration Management • Product Issues Management, • Change Control and Traceability,		

Note:
1. All processes concerned input/output, linkage, resource, criteria, Management/metrics/measurement, improvement will be assessed at each process audit stage;
2. The and processes owners must be available for audit.
3. Audit plan will be revised subject to situation on site.
4. Audit plan may be changed based on the performance review results.

Appendix 5 – Sample of Internal Quality Audit Checklist

Company Logo

QUALITY AUDIT CHECKLIST

Date: _____

Name of auditors: _____

Name of auditees: _____

Procedures audited: _____

Clauses audited: ISO 9001:2008 (7.5) Production and Service Provision

S/NO	CHECKLIST	OK	NC	COMMENTS
1	How does the organization implement the control of release, delivery, and post-delivery activities? Does the control include: - Production staff - Equipment and Tools - Work environment - Procedures and instructions - Materials - Packaging What QMS procedure does he/she refer to? Auditee to describe.			
2	Which distribution areas are subject to this procedure?			
3	Review evidence. What is the retention time of each quality record(s)? Does this in accordance to the documented Control of Quality Records procedure?			
4	How do you contribute to quality objectives of this company?			
5	How does the continuous improvement program roll out in this department / area / process? What are the improvements taken / conducted in this department / area / process? Auditee to describe and show applicable records.			
6	What are the metrics or KPIs in this department / area / process? How these metrics are selected? What is the status? Auditee to describe and show records.			

OK   - Acceptable
NC   - Unacceptable resulting in observation or discrepancy

PREPARED BY: _____

Appendix 6 – Sample of Internal Quality Audit Summary Report

Company Logo	

INTERNAL QUALITY AUDIT SUMMARY REPORT

Issue Date:

Audited Location/Processes:	**Head Office or (Company Location #1):** 1. Top Management 2. Business Development and Sales 3. Project Management 4. Engineering and R&D 5. Purchasing 6. Quality Management 7. Configuration Management 8. Document Control 9. Product Management 10. Customer Service 11. Material Planning 12. Human Resources 13. Infrastructure (Facilities and IT-IS) **Manufacturing or (Company Location #2):** 1. Receiving 2. Warehouse 3. Production 4. Calibration 5. Quality Control 6. ESD 7. Shipping 8. Service/Repair
Documents Title/ Revision:	Quality Manual, Quality Procedures, Work Instructions, Process Maps, Forms, Checklists, Records
Date of Audit:	Head Office: Manufacturing:
Auditor (or Audit Team):	1. Name (Lead Auditor) 2. Name(s)
Auditee(s):	All process owners, total (number) staffs
Scope of Audit:	ISO 9001:2008 Quality Management System

Audit Objectives:

This internal quality audit of the company's quality management system (QMS) was based on ISO 9001:2008 Quality Management System standard.

The audit objectives were as defined below:

1. To verify the effectiveness of the implementation of QMS documentation.
2. To verify the closure of the corrective actions and progress of opportunity for improvement identified in the last quality audits, and identify any opportunities for continuous improvement.
3. To ensure the readiness for the coming external Recertification audit (if applicable).

Audit Summary:

Auditors found the company's quality management system is effectively implemented to achieve company goals and objectives. Corrective actions identified from the last internal audit have been verified and closed. Most opportunities for improvement identified from the last audits have been closed. Some of them require longer time frame to capture more supporting evidence.

Page 1 of 2

1. Summary of Positive Results and Strengths

Overall, during Internal audit the auditors identified the following strengths:

- Top Management commitment is clearly seen to effective implementation of QMS.
- Strong leadership, understanding and support on Quality initiatives.
- Voices of customers are more being heard, discussed, and addressed strategically.
- High cooperation and commitment from all auditees and respective staff despite their busy schedule.
- Process owners are more familiar with their respective area, responsibilities, processes and procedures.
- Successful customer quality audit result.
- Successful supplier quality audit result.

2. Summary of Findings and Non-Conformances

During the internal audit, the auditors identified the following (number) areas needing improvement.

- Head Office or Location #1: (number) non-conformance
- Manufacturing or Location # 2: (number) non-conformance

3. Summary of Opportunities for Improvement

During the internal audit, the Auditors identified (number) opportunities of improvement in order to enhance both internal and external customer satisfaction.

Corrective Action Request:

Note:
- ....

CAR#	Description	Procedure No.	Owner(s)

Opportunity for Improvement:

Note:
- ....

OFI#	Description	Procedure No.	Owner(s)

Records:

- √ Internal Audit Plan
- √ Internal Audit Checklists
- √ Internal Audit Result – Communication and Presentation (if applicable)

Submitted by:	Name (Lead Auditor)	Title
	Name (Auditor)	Title
Acknowledged by:	Name	Date
	President & CEO	

Winning the Audit   141

Appendix 7 – Sample of Corrective and Preventive Action Report Form

Company Logo

Form-05
Quality Management
Version XX, MM/DD/YYYY

Corrective and Preventive Action Report		
Issue Date:	CAR Number:	CAR Originator:
Product:		CAR Owner:
Product Number:		Quality Rep.:
Process:		Engineering Rep.:
Location(s):		Production Rep.:
Problem Definition		
Description:		
Impact: (Quantity, Lot Number, Manufacturing Number, Value in $)		
Root Cause Analysis		
Root Cause:		
Corrective and Preventive Actions		
Corrective Action(s):		
Preventive Action(s):		
Monitoring and Control(s):		
Verification and Closure		
Quality Rep. Comments:		
CAR Status:	☐ Closed	☐ Require further monitoring
CAR Close Date:	Approval by Quality Rep:	
	(Name)	(Signature)

Quality Terms and Definitions

Accreditation – Formal recognition of an organization's technical competency to perform specific tests, type of tests, or calibration.

Appraisal – A form of the quality system audit, normally conducted to examine the total quality program effectiveness and implementation. An appraisal is usually conducted by a third-party and reported to highest management level.

Assessment – An estimate or determination of the significance, importance, and value of something.

Attribute – A characteristic or property that is appraised in terms of whether it does or does not exist, with respect to a given requirement.

Audit – A planned, independent, and documented assessment to determine whether agreed upon requirements are met.

Audit Program – The organizational structure, commitment, and documented methods used to plan and perform audits.

Audit Team – The group of individuals conducting an audit under direction of a team leader.

Audit Team Leader – The individual who supervises auditors during an audit.

Auditee – An organization or person to be (being audited).

Auditing Organization – A unit or function that carries out audits through its employees. This organization may be a department of the auditee, a client, an independent third party.

Auditor – The individual who carries out the audit.

Auditor (Quality) – A person who has the qualifications to perform quality audit.

Batch – A definite quantity of some product or material produced under conditions that are considered uniform.

Benchmarking – The process of comparing one's business processes and performance metrics to industry bests or best practices from other industries.

Best practice – A method or technique that has consistently shown results superior to those achieved with other means, and that is used as a benchmark. In addition, a "best" practice can evolve to become better as improvements are discovered. Best practice is considered by some as a business buzzword, used to describe the process of developing and following a standard way of doing things that multiple organizations can use.

Calibration – A comparison of two instruments or measuring devices one of which is a standard of known accuracy traceable to national standards – to detect, correlate, report, or eliminate by adjustment any discrepancy in accuracy of the instrument measuring device being compared to the standard.

Certification – The procedure and action, by a duly authorized body, of determining, verifying, and attesting in writing to the qualifications of personnel, processes, procedures, or items in accordance with applicable requirements.

Characteristic – A property that helps to identify or to differentiate between entities and that can be described or measured to determine conformance or nonconformance to requirements.

Client – The person or organization that has the authority to initiate an audit. Depending on the circumstances, the client may be the auditing organization, the auditee, or a third-party.

Compliance – An affirmative indication or judgment that the supplier (of the product or service) has met the requirements of the relevant specifications, contract, or regulation; also the state of meeting the requirements.

Confirmation – The concurrence of data or information obtained from two or more different sources.

Conformance – An affirmative indication or judgment that a product or service has met the requirements of the relevant specifications, contract, or regulation; also the state of meeting the requirements.

Conformity – Meet or compliant with requirements.

Concession (Quality) – A written authorization to accept (with or without repair) a product with a major/critical nonconformity, a nonconformity affecting the cosmetic appearance of the product or a nonconformity affecting the next assembly of the product delivered as subassembly/assembly.

Contractor – Any organization under contract to furnish items or services; a vendor, supplier, subcontractor, fabricator, and sub-tier levels of these where appropriate.

Correction – Any action that is taken to eliminate nonconformity. However, corrections do not address causes. When applied to products, corrections can include reworking products, reprocessing them, regarding them, assigning them to a different use, or simply destroying them.

Corrective Action – Action taken to eliminate the root cause(s) and symptom(s) of an existing undesirable deviation or nonconformity to prevent recurrence.

Corrective Action Request – A formal document noting audit findings and requesting resolution.

Customer – Anyone who receives products or services from a supplier organization. Customers can be people or organizations and can be either external or internal to the supplier organization.

Customer Satisfaction – A customer perception. It can vary from high satisfaction to low satisfaction. If customers believe that you have met their requirements, they experience high satisfaction. If they believe that you have not met their requirements, they experience low satisfaction.

Customer Property – Any property that is owned (or provided) by the customer.

Defect – A departure of a quality characteristic from its intended level that occurs with a severity sufficient to cause an associate product or service not to satisfy intended normal, or reasonably foreseeable, usage requirements.

Defective – A unit of product or service containing at least one defect or having several imperfections that in combination cause the unit not to satisfy intended normal, or reasonable foreseeable, usage requirements.

Deviation – A non-conformance of a product or a departure of characteristic from specified product, process, or system requirements.

Design and Development – A process (or a set of processes) that uses resources to transform requirements (inputs) into characteristics or specifications (outputs) for products, processes, and systems.

Effectiveness – The degree to which a planned effect is achieved. Planned activities are effective if these activities are realized. Similarly, planned results are effective if these results are actually achieved.

Efficiency – A relationship between results achieved (outputs) and resources used (inputs). Efficiency can be enhanced by achieving more with the same or fewer resources. The efficiency of a process or system can be enhanced by achieving more or getting better results (outputs) with the same or fewer resources (inputs).

Evaluation – The act of examining a process or group to some standard and forming certain conclusions as a result.

Evidence – Something that furnishes proof. An outward sign or indication. Facts that is verifiable.

Examination – A measurement of goods or services to determine conformance to some specified requirement.

Exit Meeting – the meeting at the end of the audit between the auditors and the representative auditees, at which time a rough draft of audit findings and observations is presented.

Finding – A conclusion of importance based on observation9s). An evaluation of audit evidence against audit criteria.

Guideline – A documented instruction that is considered good practice but that is not mandatory.

Independence – Freedom from bias and external influences.

Infrastructure - The entire system of facilities, equipment, and services that an organization needs in order to function includes buildings and workspaces (including related utilities), process equipment (both hardware and software), support services (such as transportation and communications), and information systems.

Inspection – Activities such as measuring, examining, and testing that gauge one or more characteristics of a product or service and the comparison of these with specified requirements to determine conformity. Inspection is a planned activity in the production process.

Key Performance Indicator (KPI) – A metric or measure. KPIs are used to quantify and evaluate organizational success. They measure how much success you've had and how much progress you've made relative to the objectives you wish to achieve. KPIs are also used to set measurable objectives, evaluate progress, monitor trends, make improvements, and support decision making. KPIs should be quantifiable and appropriate and should collect information that is useful to your organization and relevant to the needs and expectations of interested parties.

Lead Auditor – the individual who supervises auditors during an audit as a team leader.

Management – All the activities that are used to coordinate, direct, and control an organization.

Management Review – An evaluation of the suitability, adequacy, and effectiveness of an organization's quality management system, and to look for improvement opportunities.

Mission – A statement explains why an organization exists. It defines its reason for being.

Noncompliance – A departure from minimum requirements specified in a contract, specification, drawing, etc.

Non-conformance – A parameter which does not meet its specification. A departure of quality characteristics from its intended level, severe enough to create a departure from specification requirements.

Nonconforming Product – A product containing at least one nonconformity.

Nonconformity – The non-fulfillment of specified requirements.

Objective Evidence – Qualitative or quantitative information, records, or statements of fact pertaining to the quality of an item or service or to the existence and implementation of a quality system element, which is based on observation, measurement, or test and which can be verified.

Observation – A statement of fact made during an audit and substantiated by objective evidence.

Outsourced Process – Any process that is part of your organization's quality management system (QMS) but is performed by a party that is external to your organization.

Organization -

Entrance Meeting – Opening meeting or pre-audit meeting – the introductory meeting between the auditors and the representative auditees, at which time the overview of the planned audit is presented.

Procedure – A document that specifies the way to perform activity.

Process – The particular method of producing a product or service, generally involving a number of steps or operations.

Product – A piece of goods manufactured for a customer or service delivered to a customer.

Product Realization – All phases of the development of a product, including idea, design, prototype, and production. It refers to all the processes that are used to bring products into being.

Quality – The degree to which a set of inherent characteristics fulfill requirements. The totally of features and characteristics of a product, activity, or system that bears on its ability to satisfy stated or implied needs.

Qualification – The status given to an entity or person when the fulfillment of specified requirements has been demonstrated. It is the process of obtaining that status.

Audit Method – The audit verification activities used to obtain objective information essential to provide evidence of merit to qualify the audit conclusions.

Quality Assurance – Planned and systematic actions necessary to provide adequate confidence that a product or service will satisfy give quality requirements.

Quality Audit – A systematic and independent examination and evaluation to determine whether quality activities and results comply with planned arrangements and whether there arrangements are implemented effectively and are suitable to achieve objectives.

Quality Control – The operational techniques and activities that are used to fulfill requirements for quality.

Quality Management – the totality of functions involved in the determination and achievement of quality.

Quality Management System – The organizational structure, responsibilities, procedures, processes, and resources for implementing quality management.

Quality Manual – A document stating the quality policy, quality system, and quality practices of an organization.

Quality Objectives - A quality oriented goals that are generally based on or derived from an organization's quality policy and must be consistent with it. They are usually formulated at all relevant levels within the organization and for all relevant functions.

Registration – When an accredited third-party assesses the management system and issues a certificate to show that the organization abides by the principles set out in a quality system standard such as ISO 9001:2008.

Record – A type of document that provide evidence that activities have been performed or results have been achieved.

Requirement – A need, expectation, or obligation. It can be stated or implied by an organization, its customers, or other interested parties.

Root Cause – A fundamental deficiency that results in a non-conformance and must be corrected to prevent recurrence of the same or similar non-conformance.

Sample – A group of units or observations taken from a larger collection of units or observations that serves to provide an information basis for making a decision concerning the larger quantity.

Self-Assessment – A comprehensive and systematic review of an organization's overall maturity and is used to help achieve and sustain organizational success.

Specification – The document that prescribes the requirements with which the product or service must conform.

Standard – The documented result of a particular standardization effort approved by a recognized authority.

Standardization – The act of documenting, formalizing, and implementing efforts which result in an improvement, (for the purpose of conformity), to similar or applicable processes or systems.

Standard Operating Procedure – A document describing an organization process. It contains a moderate amount of detail.

Strategy – A logically structured plan or method for achieving long term goals.

Survey – An examination for some specific purpose; to inspect or consider carefully; to review in detail. (Note: some authorities use the words "audit" and "survey" interchangeably. Audit implies the existence of agreed upon criteria against which the plans and execution can be checked. Survey implies the inclusion of matters not covered by agreed upon criteria).

Top Management – A person or a group of people at the highest level within an organization. It refers to the people who coordinate, direct, and control organizations.

Value - The general principles and beliefs that are important to your organization.

Verification – The act of reviewing, inspecting, testing, checking, auditing, or otherwise establishing and documenting whether items, processes, services, or documents conform to specified requirements.

Vision – A statement that describes what the organization wants to be and how it wants to be seen by interested parties.

Work Environment – A working conditions. It refers to all of the conditions and factors that influence work.

Work Instruction – A document describing specific activities and tasks within the organization. It contains the greatest amount of detail.

References

1. International Organization for Standardization, *ISO 9001:2008 Quality Management Systems - Requirements,* Fourth Edition, 2008.
2. J.P. Russell, *The ASQ Auditing Handbook*, Third Edition, ASQ Quality Audit Division, ASQ Quality Press, Milwaukee, 2005.
3. Jack Griffin, *How to Say It Best*, Prentice Hall, 1994.
4. Rosalie Maggio, *The Art of Talking to Anyone*, McGraw-Hill, 2005.
5. Pam F. Anderson, Bill L. Wortman, *CQA Primer – The Quality Auditor Primer*, Sixth Edition, Quality Council of Indiana, 2004.
6. Glen Gee, Wesley R. Richardson, Bill L. Wortman, *CMQ Primer – The Manager of Quality Primer*, Sixth Edition, Quality Council of Indiana, 2005.
7. Susah H. Gebelein, Kristie J. Nelson-Neuhaus, Carol J. Skube, David G. Lee, Lisa A. Stevens, Lowell W. Hellervik, Brian L. Davis, *Successful Manager's Handbook*, Seventh Edition, Personnel Decisions International, 2004.
8. Russell T. Westcott, *The Certified Manager of Quality Organizational Excellence Handbook*, Third Edition, Quality Management Division, American Society of Quality, AQ Quality Press, Milwaukee, 2006.

About The Author

Monika Nonce Ardianto CQA, CQM, is a certified quality auditor and certified manager of quality / operational excellence.

Monika has over 20 years of various experiences in the leadership and supervision of the development and implementation of ISO 9001 quality management system, supplier quality management, the development of quality control plan, managing internal, customer and third party audits, handling customer complaint, project management, product configuration management, document control, laboratory management, manufacturing, and operations in pulp and paper, waste water treatment plant, solvent purification refinery, hi-tech, navigation equipment, and oil industries.

Throughout her brilliant professional career in quality assurance and management, Monika has routinely exhibited the passion, vision and dedication necessary to be successful in the business world. She has helped companies in Singapore, Malaysia, United Kingdom, United States of America, Canada, China, Australia and Indonesia improved their quality management system and secured their highly valuable contractual agreement with their clients.

During her collegiate career, she earned a Bachelor degree in Chemical Engineering in 1991 from Bandung Institute of Technology (ITB), Indonesia.

Monika is a senior member of the American Society for Quality and has been accepted into the prestigious ranks and VIP member of Stanford Who's Who as a result of her magnificent work in the manufacturing industry.

Index

Made in the USA
Charleston, SC
10 May 2013